D0457539

THE GLOBAL BUSINESS LEADER

INSEAD Business Press Series

David Fubini, Colin Price & Maurizio Zollo
MERGERS
Leadership, Performance and Corporate Health

Manfred Kets de Vries, Konstantin Korotov
& Elizabeth Florent-Treacy
COACH AND COUCH
The Psychology of Making Better Leaders

James Teboul
SERVICE IS FRONT STAGE
Positioning Services for Value Advantage

Jean-Claude Thoenig & Charles Waldman
THE MARKING ENTERPRISE
Business Success and Societal Embedding

THE GLOBAL BUSINESS LEADER

Practical Advice for Success in a
Transcultural Marketplace

J. Frank Brown

INSEAD

Business Press

First published 2007 by
PALGRAVE MACMILLAN
Houndmills, Basingstoke, Hampshire RG21 6XS and
175 Fifth Avenue, New York, N.Y. 10010
Companies and representatives throughout the world

PALGRAVE MACMILLAN is the global academic imprint of the Palgrave Macmillan division of St. Martin's Press, LLC and of Palgrave Macmillan Ltd. Macmillan® is a registered trademark in the United States, United Kingdom and other countries. Palgrave is a registered trademark in the European Union and other countries.

ISBN-13: 978-0-230-52215-2
ISBN-10: 0-230-52215-7

This book is printed on paper suitable for recycling and made from fully managed and sustained forest sources. Logging, pulping and manufacturing processes are expected to conform to the environmental regulations of the country of origin.

A catalogue record for this book is available from the British Library.

A catalog record for this book is available from the Library of Congress.

10   9   8   7   6   5   4   3   2   1
16   15   14   13   12   11   10   09   08   07

Printed and bound in China

This book is dedicated to the memory of my father, Joseph Brown, who showed me, by the way he lived his life each day, just the right measures of professionalism, compassion and good sense to be successful in life while maintaining a pretty good sense of values along the way. My only wish is that he could have been around to share some of the last 23 years. Dad, we would have had a blast!

CONTENTS

CONTENTS

ACKNOWLEDGEMENTS

So many people to thank for their help in the preparation of this book – and in the development of my thoughts on leadership in the years that preceded it. First, my everlasting gratitude to Susan, my wife and partner in all things. And thanks, too, to Chris and Sarah, two of the greatest children anyone could ask for; my mother, Elizabeth, and my brother, Bob, who have always been there for me; and my father-in-law, Bob Stoner, who has been both a great example of a leader and a mentor to me for the past 30 years.

At the risk of forgetting someone important (my apologies if I do), I extend my sincere thanks to my colleagues and friends in the business world. I am so grateful to my colleagues at PricewaterhouseCoopers: my cofounder of Genesis Park, Bethann Brault, who helped enormously with the book; my partner and supporter in leadership development at PricewaterhouseCoopers, Rich Baird; Tom Craren, who read the manuscript and gave me some very sound advice; and all of the people at PricewaterhouseCoopers who experienced Genesis Park, particularly Amber Romine.

I must also express my gratitude to my colleagues at INSEAD: my communications team, led by Melissa Joelson, whose insights made the manuscript stronger; and Elin Williams, whose outstanding support and advice were invaluable; and to the INSEAD family, who have been incredibly welcoming and attentive to my style of leadership in our first year together.

ACKNOWLEDGEMENTS

There are a lot of people out there who have mentored me and been very good friends to me for many years. My sincere thanks to Brad Evans, George Forster, Jim Schiro, Peter Grauer, Paula Gavin, Steve Denning, Bob Ripp, Tom Leipzig and Steve Scroggins are certainly on this list; we have shared a lot with each other over the years. I have been very lucky to have mentored some outstanding people throughout my career; among them, I must thank Jim Flanagan, Kersten Lanes, Kevin Rennie, Cathrine Watkins, Matt Gorin and Todson Page for their friendship and support. You all may think that you "worked for me", but in reality we learned from each other.

This book would not have been possible without the terrific support of my editor, Karen Berman, who seemed to make all of those anecdotes sound just a little better with the turn of a phrase! And thanks, too, to the team at Cubitt, Jacobs & Prosek, my public relations firm, and especially Jen Prosek, Amy Airasian and Carrie Kalish, who have been great friends, advisors and supporters throughout this process.

I also want to thank the team at Palgrave Macmillan, and especially Stephen Rutt, who believed in this book and was of tremendous support to me.

J. Frank Brown

INTRODUCTION

We had been talking about our new international venture for nearly an hour, and we were about ready to wrap up. We had outlined our objectives and three or four key focus areas, as well as the venture's name. In fact, we had been using the name throughout our meeting. I was proud of the team, which comprised about 20 people from our offices around the globe – easily 15 different countries represented in a single meeting room. I looked at the clock, pleased that we'd be done ahead of schedule. And then I threw out my final stock question, one I had learned to ask after years of experience with international operations: "How will this idea work in your markets?"

That's when one team member, a quiet fellow from Asia, spoke: "I think it will be okay, except for the name. It means 'your ugly sister' in my part of the world."

Our little summit, flushed with productivity only a moment before, froze.

We had just dodged a major public relations disaster and we knew it. We had to come up with a new name, fast. The original name would never leave that meeting room.

Why hadn't the fellow spoken up sooner? I do recall that he was a bit jetlagged that day. But the larger answer is that, in some cultures, it would have been rude to do so. When asked, he answered. Not before.

I tell this story because it illustrates the reason for this book – the need for what I call transcultural leadership in today's global business environment. What's transcultural leadership? It's a style of running a company, or a team within a company – or any organization or institution that stretches across national borders – that combines the best practices of "traditional" business leadership with the understanding that the world is composed of many cultures whose values and customs vary dramatically. To do business globally, we need to be sensitive to these differences.

Business has been conducted internationally since the Sumerian civilization of ancient Mesopotamia began trading with other ancient states several thousand years before the birth of Christ; since then, every era has conducted business across national borders in some form or another. In our time, technology has put global business dealings within reach of many more companies, and their ranks will continue to grow. Indeed, the international orientation of the business world will become more important each time the bell rings to open the stock market for another day. Economic interdependencies are already part of that marketplace, and they will expand over time. So will international collaboration on research and development (witness the developments in the field of alternative energy, for example). Whether you sell goods and services abroad; conduct manufacturing operations "offshore"; outsource technical support or other functions; or procure raw materials on the international market, it simply won't be possible to disregard the transcultural leadership imperative.

This doesn't mean that the transcultural leader must be fluent in 30 languages or expert in the manners and mores that go with them. Hardly. But he or she must know how to function in the places where those languages are spoken, must know how to get up to speed on the customs and values that pertain to each deal or transaction – must, in short, have the experience and the mindset to work in and across different cultures. That said, I'm continually surprised at the many businesspeople who don't even try. They're locked into a nineteenth-century model, and seem happy to be there. Well into the twentieth century, too many Western businesspeople approached international ventures from this nineteenth-century mindset – that is, with the idea of ramming "their way" down the local peoples' throats. I submit that this approach is intellectually and financially bankrupt. In the twenty-first century, the successful transcultural leader will use all the tools of contemporary business and combine them with a sensitivity to cultural differences. And that's why I've written this book.

What qualifies me as an expert on the concept of transcultural leadership? First, I could point out that at INSEAD, the international business school where I am the Dean, our mission is not only to teach a rigorous and up-to-the-minute business curriculum, but to create a diverse community of faculty and students from around the world who can engage with that curriculum in an atmosphere of real cultural interchange. The goal – which I must add predates my arrival, but which I wholeheartedly embrace – is that the 900 MBA candidates who pass through our program each year emerge from their studies with a unique global perspective that combines the most sophisticated business knowledge with cultural sensitivity and awareness. With more than 70 nationalities represented and no single one representing more than 12 per cent of the class, INSEAD truly develops leaders who have an appreciation and understanding of cultural diversity and an ability to operate in an international marketplace.

My interest in leadership, and more specifically transcultural leadership, really began years ago; when I look back, I realize that I've been studying the subject informally for most of my 25-plus years in the business world, and perhaps even before that. But my first experience with leadership I owe to my father.

My father, Joseph Brown, was a relationship officer (really a vice president) at a bank in suburban New Jersey, US, where we lived. He was a calm, friendly man who knew his clients and cared about them, and they loved and respected him in return. During his career, he financed shoe stores, furniture stores, a rabbinical college, a trucking company; you name it. He was never a CEO – to my everlasting sadness, he died young – but he was definitely a leader within his company and in our community. When I entered the corporate world, I modeled my style on his. And as my personal trajectory took me upward in rank and outward to an increasingly international clientele, I built on the foundation I'd absorbed from him.

I started out as an auditor at a New York bank. Two years later, I moved to the accounting firm of Price Waterhouse. I spent a fascinating 26 years in various divisions at the company, which, after a merger, came to be known as PricewaterhouseCoopers. It was a wonderful time to be part of a major accounting firm, because it was the era of mergers and acquisitions, and I had the opportunity to work on an amazing variety of interesting and important deals, many of which were international in nature and obliged me to travel widely. Since my first trip (to the Netherlands, in 1981), I've spent time in the major capitals of Europe, Asia and Australia, as well as North and South America and Africa – 37 countries in all. As a result, I've had the rare and privileged opportunity to observe the workings of businesses and their leaders around the world.

During those years, too, I learned about leadership on the job, through trial and error. The first time I was asked to direct a unit within Price Waterhouse, I was a young second-year partner eager to do well. I didn't have much formal leadership training and I worried whether anyone, particularly the older, more experienced members of the team, would want to follow me. What I found was that the entire team wanted and needed a leader; they had been struggling without a real chief for some time, and they were hungry for someone to lead them, someone who could move them to work together toward a common goal, but who was, at the same time, open to their ideas – the very things I'd learned from my dad. I approached the job as if I had as much to learn as to teach – a strategy that has served me well throughout my career. Of course, with each new project and each new goal, I added to my leadership "toolkit" and "downloaded" more information and observations into my mental catalog of what does – and does not – make for a good leader. And with each new project and each new goal, I became more firmly convinced that organizations must consciously develop their leaders and that such development programs should start early and should reflect the diverse cultural makeup of the workforce and the marketplace.

The more I've observed, the more positive I've become that organizations need leaders at every level – not just at the top, but for every team or department that makes up the whole. We need leaders to train new employees, to set the right example, right from the start. We need leaders to interact with clients and constituents, and to represent the organization in the community. Any part of the organization that lacks leaders is a weak link, and that goes from the boardroom to the maintenance staff. Imagine what would happen if a company staged a major event to celebrate its 100th anniversary, and on the big night, with a thousand or so guests in evening clothes seated and ready, the fancy media presentation cued up and the CEO standing at the lectern to speak – imagine what would happen if the circuits blew and the whole place was plunged into darkness. And imagine if it turned out that the team "leader" for the event had neglected to meet with the building ops manager to discuss logistics. Organizations need leaders at every level, and they need to train them early, not when they receive their promotions.

A few years ago, I got a chance to put my ideas on leadership into practice at PricewaterhouseCoopers. In 2000, I had moved from the position of managing partner of the New York office to that of global leader of the audit business. A threefold imperative – to innovate, to build dynamic teams and to motivate young people to stay with the firm – was clear. I was mulling how to proceed, when, during a break at a meeting in Rome, I met up with Bethann Brault, then assistant to the CEO. We got to talking about these issues, and kept talking in the months after that meeting. The result was that she and I developed Genesis Park, a five-month residential leadership development program, for the firm. Each year, some 60 or so PricewaterhouseCoopers up-and-comers rotate in and out of the program, which, since its inception in 2001, has hosted more than two hundred participants from offices in some 40 countries. I regularly spent time there, talking with these future leaders, and it was through these talks, both formal and informal, that I honed my concept of the transcultural leader. Around this time, too, I got involved with INSEAD, first because PricewaterhouseCoopers had contracted with the school to research high-performing organizations (I was the liaison) and later, as a member of the school's various advisory boards. I was happy to serve in this capacity because I've always believed that there is a vital link between education and leadership. I was particularly impressed with INSEAD because its mission mirrors my own contention that businesses and organizations must be more diverse if they are to succeed in today's world. I became more and more involved in the school and in late 2005, I was appointed Dean.

This book is the result of all these experiences. It is aimed at young people aspiring to leadership in the business world – perhaps those applying to graduate school, or just finishing their studies – and to the young journeymen (or women) executives who hope to attain leadership positions. It might also appeal to those who seek to lead complex organizations outside the business world. It might even help those who already hold leadership positions and are seeking a better understanding of transcultural leadership issues. Whatever your goals, if you are reading this book, you likely understand that we live in a time when the old style of business as usual is just too old and out of date. The need for transcultural leaders has never been greater. The good news is that navigating the international business landscape is not a burden. In fact, it's fascinating and fun if you keep yourself open to new experiences and are always ready to learn. Openness is the key to success – in business and in life.

PART I

THOUGHTS ON LEADERSHIP

Many people aspire to leadership. It's a shame that they don't focus on what leadership means. Or what it requires. Because, unlike wealth or celebrity, true leadership does require a lot from those who would achieve it. And what is required is not always what the aspirants think.

1

WHAT'S A TRANSCULTURAL LEADER ANYWAY?

When I began to write this book, I opened my dictionary to look up the word "leader", just to see how its editors' definition would compare to mine. I found all sorts of quirky tidbits: I learned that a leader can be the shoot of a plant; a newspaper editorial or a blank section at the beginning or end of a reel of film, among other things. Interesting, but none too useful for my purposes. Another entry defines a leader as one who leads or a guide or conductor or one who has commanding authority. Getting warmer, but these phrases still don't do justice to a word that, in my view, should convey volumes. Simply having – or even commanding – authority does not make a person a leader. When I closed the book, it occurred to me that it's probably easier to define what a leader is not. A person is not a leader because he or she happens to hold a high rank or title, or occupy a corner office. A true leader might, in fact, do both, but there are plenty of people with impressive titles on their business cards and football-field-sized offices who are not leaders. I like to call these folks LINOs – Leaders In Name Only. LINOs typically get their positions by concentrating primarily on their own advancement – not on the job at hand, not on the good of the organization they work in and not on the welfare of their colleagues. Once in place, they hold on for dear life by surrounding themselves with yes-men – mirror-image managers who do their bidding without question or challenge. LINOs believe this is the way to maintain control, but it's actually a myopic strategy that has left many a company and organization unprepared to face the challenges posed by our fast-changing world. At its worst, this way of doing business has resulted in many of the cases of corruption that have preoccupied the nightly news in recent years. Open any newspaper and you'll find LINOs on every other page, in business, and in politics, too. They lack backbone and conviction about any topic other than the preservation of their jobs and the perks that go with them. They might make the cut into the dictionary definition of a leader, but not mine.

HALLMARKS OF LEADERSHIP

At the most fundamental level, a true leader must guide others to accomplish the work of the organization. How he perceives that work, and the spirit in which she offers that guidance, are key. Here are a few of the hallmarks of true leaders as I have observed them:

- **The leader must be open**. Only through openness can he or she learn enough to make informed decisions, adopt innovative ideas, get warning of obstacles ahead and otherwise stay attuned to the world outside the organization. I don't think you can be a leader if you believe there's only one way (your way) to do something. And openness goes both ways. Not only must the leader be open to hearing from the team, he or she must also share openly with them. It's imperative for a leader to be willing to have a dialogue, to answer questions straightforwardly. (And if you can't answer at a given moment, be honest about that, too.)

- As a corollary, the leader must forge teams comprising the most diverse group of people possible to ensure that their work is grounded in the broadest possible spectrum of information.

■ **A leader must embody integrity and inspire trust.** If you want to motivate people to follow you and get the job done, you'll do best if they trust and respect you and know that you are being honest with them.

- As a corollary, you must cultivate your memory, so that you can make good on your promises. (Diaries, in whatever form, are a big help, as is a good assistant.)

■ **A leader must understand his or her own and his or her organization's objectives.** Only with clear knowledge of these objectives can he or she set goals for the team that are high but achievable.

- As a corollary, the leader must know how to set goals and make decisions based on consultation with his or her team. Once the decisions are made, he or she must know how to implement them.

■ **A leader must have an optimistic, can-do outlook.** Nothing is worse for motivating the troops than a leader with a bad attitude. By contrast, assuming a leader has set achievable goals, a can-do attitude can set the tone for the team's labors and secure their emotional investment in getting the job done.

- As a corollary, a leader must guard against rose-colored-glasses syndrome. If obstacles emerge, the leader must not brush them off with false optimism but, rather, work with the team to devise ways to overcome them.

- **A leader must know how to use and not abuse author-ity.** He or she must respect others in the organization, whatever their rank.
  - As a corollary, the leader must be aware that all members of the team have personal lives as well as work lives and that the two must be balanced.

- **A leader must cultivate humility.** He or she must recognize that work gets done by teams, so credit must be shared. A leader should be able to recognize his or her team publicly and often.
  - As a corollary, a leader should have a sense of humor, a trait that is often overlooked. Being able to share a laugh and not take yourself too seriously is a great plus in motivating a team.

- **The leader must consider not just the present, but the future.** He or she must therefore focus on the careers of others in the organization and must actively foster their development, both by mentoring individuals and by creating an atmosphere where professional growth is prized and people are encouraged to take on new challenges.
  - As a corollary, the leader must ultimately put in place a workable succession plan.

These are the hallmarks of business leadership. Too long for a dictionary definition, I'm afraid, but there they are. And there's more to add.

A decade or two ago, the above might have been enough, but as I've said earlier, the marketplace is not what it was a decade or two ago. Increasingly, business is conducted across national borders by parties whose cultural values and customs are dramatically different. Countries once known as "third world" or "developing" are stepping up to take a larger, more assertive role on the world stage, and the old assumption that their people will passively accept conditions imposed on them by Western nations no longer holds, if it ever did. At the same time, divisions within the West are more and more apparent. This is why I contend that we need not just leaders, but transcultural leaders. And so I must add the following to the qualities listed above:

- **The transcultural leader is sensitive to national and cultural differences.** He or she factors these differences into his or her business dealings.
  - As a corollary, the transcultural leader knows that there is much *to know* and knows how and where to get advice on moving around and doing business in unfamiliar locales.

THE TRANSCULTURAL ANGLE

What do this last bullet point and its corollary mean in practical terms? I've seen this concept go right to the bottom line. Neglect cultural issues and, as would be the case if you neglected any other aspect of the transaction at hand, you might imperil the entire deal. I recall one case in which a deal fell through because the two sides – American and Japanese, as it happened – did not understand each other's negotiating customs. The Japanese company was interested in buying a division of an American firm. The Japanese team did extensive due diligence, but was reluctant to make an offer because their valuation of the business was below the "expected price" as communicated by the seller's investment banker. The Japanese company assumed that the Americans would be offended by the lower bid, as would have been the case in their country. The Americans, on the other hand, assumed that the Japanese would make a bid and then negotiate. I was the advisor to the Japanese company and I spent hours explaining the way such deals worked in the United States: the prospective buyer makes an offer and then both parties follow up with a negotiation. I was ready to fly to Tokyo to explain it to their top management. My counterparts on the American side did not want to hear about cultural differences. They were motivated to sell, sure, but they just assumed that they would get multiple bids and didn't want to listen to me or my clients until it was too late. So what could have been a mutually beneficial deal never happened.

How do you avoid this kind of cultural fiasco? I can speak from my own experience and say that, over the years, I learned never to go into a place that was new to me without first finding out how to properly conduct a meeting there, how to get the salutations and courtesy titles right, how to deal with seating, dining, coffee/tea etiquette and, of course, how to make and respond to an offer in a negotiation. I learned, too, to go beyond the dos and don'ts of your business agenda and learn about how things are done in daily life there. Do you, for example, tip for service? If so, how much? Do you shake hands on meeting? Bow? Or perhaps kiss each cheek twice? What are the social graces that are unique to the place? (In Japan, it's customary, during a meal, to fill the drinking glasses of your companions and then wait for one of them to fill yours.)

It's useful – and personally rewarding – to experience different cultures. If you are in a foreign land, don't look for a restaurant that serves food from home; try the local fare. Watch some local TV; you might not speak the language, but you'll glean a lot from the pictures and the presentation, and you might even pick up a word or two that will impress your hosts. If you have time, attend a cultural or sporting event. Venture beyond your hotel and do a little shopping in the marketplace. Get a haircut. Every new transaction will teach you something about the culture you're dealing in.

I've also learned to find out a bit about the local history, culture and current politics. It's useful to know who the president or prime minister is, when the next election will take place, who the political parties are – whatever is germane to the particular nation in which you are doing business. These might seem like small matters, but getting them wrong can start you off on the wrong foot, while making the effort to get them right will help you put your best foot forward.

These gestures are helpful not just in dealing with the people on the other side of the conference table, but on your side, too, because you will likely employ people who live in the country where you're doing business. Your workforce might range from a single assistant/translator to an entire branch office. Whatever the size of the team, you'll find that its members can help you learn the local customs, and you'll likely win their loyalty and respect when you show them you take their culture seriously.

When I think back to the American–Japanese deal that fell through, I return to my first hallmark of leadership: openness. As our reach out into the world expands and international exchanges proliferate, this quality will become all the more important. Openness to listen to the team you are leading, openness to your colleagues across the negotiating table, openness to the country you've flown across the globe to do business in – all will be vital to your success. LINOs might think they can stay closeted in their offices and wing it; leaders – true leaders, that is – know there's no margin in it.

2

THE VALUE OF VALUES

One of the best tips for the aspiring leader comes from that well-known business guru, William Shakespeare. I'm thinking of the much-quoted line from *Hamlet*: "This above all: to thine own self be true."

Today, some might read that as a carte blanche for looking out for number one, but I think it's more meaningful as a reminder to be clear about what you believe; to know the kind of person – the kind of leader – you want to be; to understand the difference between right and wrong, and to have a firm idea of what is nonnegotiable for you. Over the years, I've adopted the term "mirror test" to describe this. I'm sure you've heard similar phraseology – it boils down to a question: Can I look at myself in the mirror and know I've done the right thing? I've also called it the "front-page meter", although, these days, I might substitute *YouTube* for front-page. Whatever the medium, the point is the same: Would I be proud to see this reported in the press? What would the rest of the world conclude about me and my business dealings?

I guess what I'm talking about are values. It might not be fashionable to devote an entire chapter to this subject in a business book, but I can't conceive of talking about leadership without giving values a prominent place. If you begin each day armed with a sense of what's important and what's nonnegotiable, the mirror test and *YouTube* meter moments will be easier to navigate. (Notice that I didn't say easy. Business often requires difficult and painful decisions. One day, you might decide whether to trust a particular business associate; another, you'll rule on whether to accept or reject a deal. One day, you'll determine whether a well-meaning but misplaced individual will lose his or her job; another, whether you'll lay off a few thousand. Your sense of what's important will ensure that you do what you do for the right reasons.)

This doubtless sounds idealistic – and it is. Yet, as much as I encourage you to embrace the idealistic notion of holding true to your values, I must also warn against misplaced idealism. What I mean is: Never assume that the rest of the world will share your values. Hope that they will, but don't count on it. This is not an ideal world. If it were, no one would ever lie, steal, or even hide the truth. In an ideal world, all competition would be friendly and no one would ever do anything to harm a competitor, all contracts would be awarded fairly and all promotions would be based on merit. But this is not an ideal world, so the question remains: What are my nonnegotiables? In these days of ethical breaches, governance lapses and scandals du jour, it's important to work that out for yourself before the test comes up.

VALUES IN A MULTICULTURAL ENVIRONMENT

Dealing in a multicultural environment, the whole question of values becomes even more complex. You'll find soon enough that different cultures don't share the same values or business practices. A termination or layoff that might be a routine business decision in the United States would be unacceptable in Germany, where a Works Council, not management, decides who will be laid off. Likewise, what would be labeled a bribe in some places might be just a "gift" elsewhere – a normal part of doing business. In my auditing days, I heard about this kind of thing often enough from clients who had to pay a "gift" in order for their shipments to get to port. Yet another example: the pace of business varies from place to place. People from the United Kingdom might do well to be a bit more aggressive in the United States, while Americans might have to slow down and be less aggressive in the United Kingdom.

In Korea and India, I had the experience of asking to meet with young staff people, only to have the senior people ask why. The cultures of both countries placed such great value on seniority that my colleagues couldn't imagine what I could possibly learn from the younger staff. In the end, I persisted and in both places I was able to meet with some junior staff members, but I was careful to do so while showing respect for the senior people and, afterward, I shared with them what I had learned. In Korea, for example, it was commonplace to come to the office on Saturday, whether or not there was work to do. When I told the senior partner there that the younger generation was questioning this practice, he, to his credit, changed the policy.

There will be times when a clash of cultures will not be so easy to iron out. The treatment of women and minority groups is a particularly difficult issue in some places. There's no easy answer. You're not going to change an entire culture, but you must decide the degree to which you will participate in it – or not. And you must figure out what aspects of the situation you have the power to influence. I think prejudice is something a leader just has to fight against. There are times when you can't go along with the local custom. But there are ways to do this respectfully. In cases where differences seem

13

unbridgeable and tempers start to show, I always ask for a time-out to let everyone cool down. And I try to be subtle and calm, but persuasive and persistent. Persistence is what creates the win-win; people usually come around. If you are clear on your own values – and what's nonnegotiable – you'll always have that as your touchstone.

VALUES IN YOUR PERSONAL LIFE

Your values will determine more than your business dealings; they will determine the course of your personal life and the inevitable spillover in between the two. So it's vital to think about what's really important to you. Do you want a family? A fat bankbook? A high-powered job? What will each of those goals require? Which would you sacrifice, if you couldn't have it all? Or, in a more optimistic light, how will you balance the conflicting demands that they will make?

These are profound questions. I think regular personal planning – based on your deepest values and your dearest goals – is imperative. Each year, sit down and think about what you want your life to look like in the coming months. Write it all down and return to it periodically. Ask yourself questions such as:

- What kind of organization do I want to work for?

- What kind of education do I need?

- How much money do I need? Want?

- Do I want a family?

- Do I want to be a leader?

14

Think carefully about your answers to these questions and prioritize your most important goals. Choose a few to focus on each year. Resist the temptation to be too specific. "I want to obtain experience in Asia" is probably a better goal than "I want to spend six months in Indonesia." The former can be accomplished in a number of ways and leaves you open to opportunities that you might never have imagined in writing your plan. Beware; your plan will change over time. If you are just starting out, getting the right job might take precedence over starting a family. A few years later, however, your priorities might reverse themselves. Or not. Only you can figure that out.

For me – and I suspect for many of the readers of this book – family will always be a priority, and I've always tried to balance my home and work lives. I've been lucky to have had bosses who shared this value. I'll always remember one day in 1997, right in the middle of the Price Waterhouse– Coopers & Lybrand merger. I was on the Price Waterhouse board and had been fairly involved in the lead-up to the merger. The final vote of the board was to take place on a Monday. My son was a high school football player at the time, and his team was scheduled to compete in an important play-off game the weekend before the meeting. A major storm forced the postponement of the game until the Monday of the board meeting. This left me in a tough spot. I'd have to leave the board meeting early or miss the game. I went to the CEO/chairman of the board and explained my situation: I would have to leave at 3 p.m. to make it to the game. Without hesitation, he told me to go; he would hold my proxy in case I had to leave before the vote. When the time came for the meeting, something happened that I will remember for the rest of my life: intent on the discussion, I lost track of time. At 3:15, the CEO said, in front of everyone,

"Don't you have to get to your son's football game?" I excused myself and made it to the game.

I never miss a chance to tell this story, as I think it illustrates the best kind of leadership. Recently, a colleague asked me what I would have done if the CEO had told me I could not leave. Obviously, I would have stayed at the meeting and missed the game. But I wouldn't have forgotten the incident. And I probably wouldn't have stayed with the company for another eight years.

That's one of the things I'm talking about when I suggest that you ask yourself, "What kind of organization do I want to work for?" Here, let me be clear about one thing: Except in the most dire circumstances, I would never advise anyone to leave a job in anger or in haste. The question of the kind of organization you want to work for is best asked in the context of your long-term personal plan. Events might prompt you to revise your plan and seek a new employer faster than you originally anticipated, but it's usually wise to mull your options, make your inquiries and then take your leave when you've found a situation that better reflects the plan you've made for yourself.

That said, as you make your way in the world, if, above all, you stay true to your values, you'll pass the mirror test every time.

PART II

TECHNIQUES AND PRACTICES OF TRANSCULTURAL LEADERS

Some leaders are born, I suppose, but I firmly believe that most achieve their status by paying attention. That might sound like an unusual prescription for success in business, but I believe that you can and should learn something from everyone you meet – although sometimes the lessons will not be the kind you want to emulate.

One person you'll want to attend to closely is ... you. And that is the subject of this part of the book. When I recommend paying attention to oneself, I mean that you can consciously develop the techniques and practices that characterize strong transcultural leaders. You can train yourself, and in doing so, you'll be pleased to find that while these are definitely the techniques and practices of leaders, they can help anyone, at any level, to navigate the business world more effectively. Nor do they require expensive, high-tech tools or an Ivy League pedigree. They're techniques that you can make into habits – habits that will become part of who you are. The earlier you start, the better, but it's never too late to begin. You can work on cultivating these habits on your own or in conjunction with any other training you receive. And – who knows? – perhaps when you are in a position to do so, you'll develop your own leadership training program to pass along what you've learned.

3

COMMUNICATIONS

The most important attribute of a leader, as far as I'm concerned, is the ability to communicate effectively. I'm not talking about flowery language, but communications that bring your message to your audience, whoever it might be. Effective communications are essential, whether via one-on-one conversations; in print; in e-mails and other electronic communiqués; in presentations to small and large groups and whatever other possibilities lie in between. But, first, there's another aspect of communications that might seem counterintuitive: listening.

LISTENING

Listening is vital to being a leader; in fact, it's vital at any level of an organization. At its most basic, listening will provide you with information and insights on which you'll base your activities, your goals and your decision making. If you really cultivate your listening skills, however, you'll derive benefits that go far beyond information gathering.

How you listen – the quality of attention you give to people – will tell your team, your clients and everybody else how you value their input and who you are as a leader and a person. By listening well, you are also setting an example for others on your team, creating a culture in which everyone listens respectfully to everyone else. I've worked with many teams over the years and I've noticed that the most productive ones are those whose members feel as though their opinions matter, that they can make a real impact. I've also seen teams where nobody even shows up for meetings because they don't think it's worth it. "Nobody listens anyway," is the invariable refrain.

Listening to customers and constituents is equally critical. I've observed LINOs who are impatient and distracted when their customers speak – a sure way to lose business. Another kind of listening that isn't productive is what I call tick-the-box listening – making a show just to say you've done it. LINOs, when they bother to listen at all, are notorious for this listening style. They'll make grandiose gestures to show they're listening and never follow up on the information they're given. Organizations can be guilty of this, too; I've heard of companies that spend fortunes on surveys and polls, only to file them away without acting on – or even analyzing – the resulting data.

Listening can also be about what's not said. I make a point to read eye contact and engagement. And I actively solicit comments from people, both individually and in groups. This is especially important in the global arena, because, as illustrated by the international project with the unfortunate name that I mentioned in the opening of this book, in some cultures it's not polite to volunteer an opinion. Remember, too, that some team members might be reluctant to contradict a superior (a major cultural no-no in some places) or even speak up in what is not their first language. As a leader, you'll be wise to try to draw people out with questions. Take care, though, not to put people on the spot. I've developed a habit of phrasing a question that includes a ready answer just in case the person being questioned is unable to find the words. I might say, "J, I know you have been dealing with some difficult challenges, particularly with the turnover of your top staff members, but do you have any thoughts on this issue?" What I've done is given J a ready answer if that's all he or she wants to say. But what often happens is that J will be flattered that I've remembered his or her individual circumstance, and will feel comfortable enough to open up and speak.

Soliciting information is not something you do only at formal meetings. The executive who assumes that "no news from a far off branch office is good news" is the executive who will be surprised by bad news. So I always recommend seeking out information about what's going on at regular intervals.

Finally, listening begins long before that crucial piece of information reaches you. If you have created an atmosphere in which your team knows you value their insights and welcome what they have to say, they will open up and tell you what you need to know. When I was newly married, I noticed something that my father-in-law, Bob Stoner, did. He had his own manufacturing business, and every evening he left the plant through the back door. That way, he could stop and speak to every person on the shop floor on his way out. He knew each one by name, and they loved him and worked hard for him. In my career, I've tried to create the equivalent of the shop floor, even though oftentimes my "shop" has spanned several continents. A transcultural leader can get to know the players on the team by being interested. Start with the simple questions: "Tell me about your family," to the partner in Singapore. "What was your experience like at university?" to the new recruit in London. "How was your vacation?" to the staff member in Milan. I try to convey to everyone that my door is open: come in and have a chat. Not every moment; not, for example, when there's a deadline looming or a meeting in progress, but most of the time. If you show people you are open, they will approach you. And when they do, *listen*.

SPEAKING AND WRITING

While you hone your listening ability, you must also develop your spoken and written communication skills. This is particularly true when you are conducting business in a global arena. When I assumed my position as leader of the Global Audit Practice of PricewaterhouseCoopers, one of the first things I did was to draft a memo stating our strategic objectives. It probably went out to 25,000 employees around the world, and it said everything I thought needed to be said about our strategies as a global team. I thought it was pretty strong. In the months that followed, however, when I visited our offices around the world and asked people about it, I was surprised to get quite a few blank stares.

When I probed a bit, I found that my memo was flawed in three key ways. First, it wasn't as clear as I had thought. For one thing, I had used the word "assurance" to tout our firm's reliability. This was in keeping with a firmwide brand-identity initiative, but what I had forgotten was that in some places assurance means insurance – that is, I forgot this until someone asked me playfully, "Are we going into the insurance business?" We weren't, and I've never forgotten that lesson: Make sure you're using language that everyone understands.

Second, my "opus" was too long. I learned that a lot of people have a lot to read during their workdays, and if they don't get the gist of a memo early on, chances are they won't finish it. Fortunately for me, they weren't shy about telling me so.

Third, my strategic points weren't simple enough – too many long phrases, too much meandering.

Once I figured this out, I revised my "declaration" of our strategic policy, using several key phrases again and again. The policy had three components, and when I was done, all three were boiled down to less than five key words each. Within a few months, the whole team – 25,000 people – was articulating the same strategy.

Since then, I have refined my approach to communications further. Whatever mode you're dealing in – verbal or written, electronic or paper, individual or group – I recommend following these principles:

- **Be prepared:** Organize your thoughts in advance. There's nothing worse than having someone ramble along without an obvious purpose. Know the points you want to get across and state them clearly.

- **Be concise:** In most cases, if you can't craft a business communication in a few paragraphs, you're making it too complicated. I have a personal rule that no written communication should exceed one computer screen. More than that and you can't be assured that anyone will read it.

- **Be precise:** Choose your words carefully. This is particularly important in global communications, when some of your readers or listeners are receiving your message in a language that is not their native tongue. Don't force them to look up big, impressive words, and avoid jargon and acronyms. When possible, have your communications reviewed by someone familiar with the language and culture you are dealing with. (After my experience with the word "assurance", I had key memos reviewed by staff members from various locales who could clue me in to potential cultural misunderstandings.)

- **Be persistent:** Don't assume that because you've said something once, everyone will automatically remember it. You've got to stay on message, as they say in politics. Craft your message points so that they are easy to remember, and then repeat them as necessary.

- **Be passionate:** If you believe in what you're saying or writing and can show it, your audience will pick up on your passion. If you're passionate, people will listen harder, you'll motivate your team more effectively and win over your customers more easily. If you lack passion, or at the very least, interest, your message will get lost. There's no bigger turn-off than a ho-hum communicator.

I've also developed some more specific tips for various kinds of communication:

- **Spoken communications with individuals:** In a conversation between two people, I always strive for clarity and connection. Clarity, so that there are no misunderstandings, and connection, so that there's a level of trust. Eye contact is important; it's difficult to trust and relate to someone who won't look at you. It's also important to speak loudly, clearly and slowly enough to ensure that the other person comprehends what you are saying. This is especially important in a multicultural environment, so much so that I often try to subtly insert questions into my conversation to be sure that I'm being understood. In some cases, you'll have the services of a translator, and it's important to hire one who will competently and faithfully translate back and forth. (Then, too, it's good to be aware that a translator can serve purposes other than communicating in different languages. I had one client who insisted on a translator even though he spoke excellent English, because it slowed the pace of the negotiation and gave him a sense of control.)

- **Spoken communications with small groups:** In groups, the same principles apply, and it's important for the leader to set a tone that makes all present feel like their opinions and input matter. Eye contact with everyone is key. Leaders should take care not to be too "class conscious". I always like to give the most junior person as much "air time" as the most senior person. When you are doing business internationally, however, this can be tricky, as there are cultures that revere seniority to the point that they don't seek input from their juniors. In such cases, the leader can show respect for local custom by addressing the elders first, but making sure to seek input from the junior staff as well.

  Remember that different cultures encourage different levels of participation in group discussions, so do try to draw out the quiet ones. You'll also encounter the opposite challenge: the person who has an opinion on everything and talks too much. This, too, can be cultural, and it must be dealt with because it can stifle others and cause them to tune out. I generally take the direct approach, with a comment such as, "B, I think we've heard from you on this issue. Let's give someone else a chance." I have no problem doing this in the middle of B's monologue, if it has gone on long enough. I do it with a smile, but I make my point.

Of course, you need to be organized and to think about any points you want to make in advance. It can take a little practice to direct the discussion, listen to what's being said and make sure all participants have their say. So if you think you might forget something, make notes and glance at them as you go to be sure you've covered everything.

- **Written communications:** Take pains to make your writing clear. If anything, clarity is even more important in written communications, because you lack the nonverbal cues – eye contact, tone of voice and body language – that you have in a face-to-face exchange. To be sure your message gets across, you must cultivate clarity and conciseness. Cut out the extraneous and concentrate on getting to the essence of your message without making it so short that it's too vague. As I mentioned, my personal rule is to make most business communications no longer than one computer screen.

  I also avoid acronyms, as well as the abbreviations that have become fashionable lately with text messaging, as they will confuse and distance any reader who is not an insider. When you are communicating across cultures, acronyms and texting abbreviations can be deadly, because the acronym that's simple to you might mean something else in another language – or it might mean nothing at all. In cultures where asking for clarification isn't good manners, you likely won't know that your message was misunderstood until it's too late. (This goes for spoken communications, too. I once went to a meeting between my team and the client's team, which, on that day, included the client's CEO. When we went around the room introducing ourselves, one person said, "I'm with the PDS group in EMEA." I was running the meeting, so I quickly cut in and said, "Mr CEO doesn't know what that is, so let's not talk in code, now." I got a laugh, but made a point.)

- **Public speaking:** Or should I call it "The Dreaded Task of Public Speaking"? Speaking in front of larger groups scares a lot of people, and I can report that I was no exception, at first. My initial tries were somewhat harrowing, but I lived through them and I will tell you that the more you do it, the more comfortable you will become. Now I think nothing of speaking before groups numbering hundreds or thousands. And I've developed some pointers for public speaking (some of these are elaborations on the general points I began with, but they bear repeating in the context of public speaking):

  - *Plan your remarks and make notes in a form that will work for you.* Know what you plan to say. I generally work with a written list of topics. I make sure that I am thoroughly familiar with what I want to say about each item; the list itself is simply a memory aide to remind me of all the points I want to cover. You might make more detailed notes, if that makes you more comfortable. I don't, however, recommend a full script because reading a speech from the printed page rarely makes the impact that speaking extemporaneously does. I don't much like the visuals that are so popular in presentations these days because I think they can distract the audience from what you have to say, and because they can become too much of a crutch for you. If you must use slides, I suggest keeping the number low and the message on each slide simple – no more than four bullet points per slide and just one line per bullet. Simplicity

27

is particularly important, of course, with globally diverse audiences.

- *Practice your talk a few times before delivering it.* Use a stopwatch to make sure you don't exceed your allotted time. (Everyone in the room will know how long you're supposed to take; never exceed that time limit.)

- *Know the room.* One thing that novice speakers might overlook is visiting the room beforehand. Be sure that the lights and any other necessary functions work; test the microphone. If you are using visual aids, figure out how they will be placed so that the entire room can see them, and do enough run-throughs so that you are sure they will work.

- *If you are part of a larger program,* don't tune out; listen to those who speak before you. By doing so, you can refer to the other speakers and help the audience make connections. You'll also be aware of any contradictions between your presentation and those of the other speakers. It's fine to disagree, but a good speaker will gracefully acknowledge the difference with a simple "I disagree with W because…".

- *Your voice is an expressive instrument; use it.* Modulate your delivery to convey that what you are saying has meaning for your listeners. A monotone is death to the public speaker; you'll lose your audience if you sound bored by your own words. Do make yourself speak slowly and clearly enough so that your listeners can follow what you're saying; nervous public speakers tend to rush through their remarks. A slow and measured pace will actually help you keep track of what you have to say, and it can calm you as well. When you speak to more globally diverse audiences, a slower pace will help ensure that you are understood.

- *Use nonverbal cues to engage your listeners.* Move your eyes around the room; it's not possible to make eye contact with everyone in the audience as you would in a small group, but you will connect better with your listeners if you move your focus around to all areas of the room rather than just staring straight ahead. At the same time, let your body talk, too. Don't be afraid to use hand gestures and facial expressions appropriately. Try not to fall into the nervous speaker's habit of grasping the lectern woodenly or swaying unnaturally.

- *Be aware of what's happening around you.* Try to read the room as you get started and continue to do so as you go. If it's late in the day and people are tired, for example, just asking everyone to stand up and stretch for a moment or two can infuse the room with new energy. As you speak, try to be aware of the impact you are making, how effectively you're connecting with the audience and how well you're delivering your message. If necessary, modulate your presentation in response. (And don't worry if this seems like a tall order for a novice speaker; it's a skill that you develop as you go. You'll know when you're comfortable enough to pull it off.)

- *Be sensitive to multicultural audiences.* Years ago, virtually all public speakers would be given the advice to open with a joke. In a multicultural gathering, beware that your jokes might be misunderstood. I rarely if ever use a real joke; however, something easy and self-deprecating can be a good audience icebreaker. Something like this: "The organizers of today's event were looking for an expert in the area of —. Unfortunately, they couldn't find one, so you're stuck with me!" That works in almost any culture. I always recommend that Westerners be careful of telling jokes in Asia; it's not that people there don't have a sense of humor, because, of course, they do. It's just that if they don't get the joke, they'll feel embarrassed and will feel like they have to laugh – and laugh late. And then they'll feel worse. And your message will get lost.

One final thought about communications: be honest. Something I call relentless positivism has become fashionable in business communications lately. Being unnaturally positive is counter to the good leader's reliance on openness and transparency. And nobody likes a negative surprise that comes in the wake of too much positivism, not employees, not shareholders, not clients. You have to tell it straight. If there are problems, you have to say so, and then confidently say how you plan to resolve them. By doing so, you invite honesty in return. Of course, it doesn't hurt to add – in a positive tone – that you're optimistic that by working together, you'll reach a solution.

4

NETWORKING AND RELATIONSHIP BUILDING

Here's a little truth about the world: It really does matter who you know! Therefore, the twin arts of networking and developing relationships are among the most important that you can learn. In fact, networking never ends. I don't care who you are or how high you rise as a leader; you never know enough people. Networking and relationship building can help you as an individual when you seek a new job, and can help your company when you solicit new business or work to retain old business, seek financing, referrals, and recruit new talent.

Speaking personally, networking has helped me immeasurably. I got started a bit late, in my early thirties, by getting on the board of a nonprofit group. One thing led to another, and before I knew it, I was connected to three or four organizations in New York City. Then I realized something that amazed me: The organizations tended to overlap! I would go to an event sponsored by one group one week, and then another event sponsored by another group the following week, and see a lot of the same people I had seen at the previous event. With time, it became easier to walk into each room because I was confident that I would know somebody, and through that person, I would meet others. Gradually, these connections gave rise to more connections. Networking and relationship building have enabled me to meet interesting people, and helped me win business, recruit talented employees, get advice about everything from career moves to schools for my kids, get tickets to events, and more. (Notice that I say "helped me" win business. You won't stay in business by networking alone; you have to deliver your product or service. But networking certainly helps.)

The thing about networking is that you have to work at it. Like so much in life, you get out what you put in. Don't be daunted, however; networking and relationship building aren't complicated. Working at it simply means that you join one or more groups – professional or charitable – meet people and keep up with them.

When you get into the global arena, should you network? Absolutely. I think networking in some form or another is universal. But be aware that different cultures network in different ways, so, as always, do your homework. In some cultures, networking is defined by age group; senior people don't generally associate with their juniors. And some cultures are more formal than others. In the United States, for example, it's fairly common for people to entertain clients and business associates in their homes, but in other cultures, inviting a contact home would be unthinkable; for them, business entertaining takes place in restaurants. So when you start to network across cultures, do your homework, and take your cue from your networking partners.

Some further thoughts on networking and relationship building:

NETWORKING

I always tell young people to start their networking early in their careers by joining professional associations and alumni groups, and by getting out in the community by serving on the boards and committees of charities, places of worship and other organizations. The benefit of this kind of networking is not just that you meet people, which of course you do, but that you develop other leadership techniques as well. (I had my first experiences at public speaking when I served on my church board at age 25.)

I also advise people to do what I call "internal networking" at work, using much the same approach: Get on a committee, volunteer for an assignment, consider a "tour of duty" outside your home territory. Through internal networking, you'll meet more people within your organization – not just peers, but superiors as well as those of lower rank – and all of them will help you get things done and make your job more enjoyable in the process. With luck, they might also help you advance in your career.

If you achieve a leadership position, internal networking will help you build good teams and learn to identify talent. In my view, an organization that encourages internal networking, teamwork and group solutions is one that understands the path to success. It's the LINOs who encourage a "silo" mentality that breeds distrust among the troops and creates political situations that get in the way of the work at hand. Then, too, the LINO who creates obstacles to collaboration might have something to hide. If your efforts at internal networking are discouraged, you've learned something important about the company you work for, something that might figure in your plans for the future.

When I advise people to network, I always get a few stock reasons for not doing so. But none of these "reasons" stand up, and I have suggestions that can help the reluctant networker get past them:

- **"I don't know how to network."** To this I say, start where you know they need you. Nonprofit organizations are always looking for good people. Pick one that interests you and sign up. But don't stop there. The way to get the most out of the experience is to make an investment of your time and effort: Volunteer to serve on a committee (or for young people, a junior committee) or to help with a special event. When you work with people you get to know them – and they get to know you. You can also start your own organization. At PricewaterhouseCoopers, I advised a group of young professionals who were setting up their own group, which came to be known as Streetwise Partners, a very successful not for profit. It's now ten years old and going strong!

■ **"I don't have time."** When people tell me they have no time to volunteer, or can't take the time off from work, I tell them to think again. I believe that the game has changed, and most enlightened companies take the position that it's important for their people to be involved in their communities. The connections that result bring good public relations and, often enough, new business. I warn prospective volunteers, however, to do their homework. When you approach the boss, do so straightforwardly. Know how much time the commitment you're suggesting will require. Point out that it can be a win-win for you and the company. If the boss says yes, you're on your way. If you're turned down flat, then, as above, you'll learn something about your company. And it won't hurt to inquire whether another organization would be more appropriate. I had one person come back to me and say, "My boss didn't like the organization I chose, but she suggested that another group would be a better fit – and it was!"

■ **"I can't remember names."** A lot of people share this complaint. You can overcome this deficit with a little effort.

I'm told I have a knack for remembering people, but I can tell you that it's not a talent; it's focus. When I meet people, I focus on their names and something about them. I ask questions and look for memorable details in their answers. I also make sure that I put names, contact information and other details that I want to remember into my contact file promptly. It doesn't matter what kind of filing system you use. I know some people who still use revolving card files, while others have migrated to electronic databases to store their information. Just pick the kind you like best and then use it religiously.

- **"Why would they want to talk to me?"** Most people fear approaching individuals of higher rank. They feel they're not senior enough or not good enough or whatever. In all my years of networking, it's been rare that I've been rebuffed or made to feel uncomfortable. (Although discomfort can result on both sides when people approach the "big shots" feeling starstruck and don't treat them like human beings.) My advice on meeting someone of status or rank is this: Have a conversation. Assume the person will be interested in talking with you – if not, he or she would already have walked away. Get to know the person a bit; it helps if you have something interesting to say and if you know something about the person's organization and interest. Offer your business card; you might get one in return. Later, make an entry in your journal. Now, this is not to say that everyone will want to meet you – or even be civil. Some people will be focused on their own agendas, while others will simply be rude and self-absorbed (but you don't want to meet them anyway). I go by the 80/20 rule here. About 80 per cent of the people you approach will be great, and the other 20 per cent will be … the other

20 per cent. This being the case, have a strategy for working the room: When you walk up to your networking target, make sure you are near the bar or another group of people. If you need to make a hasty retreat, you can move off quickly and gracefully.

- **"I meet people, but it doesn't go anywhere."** At this stage, it's up to you. The key is to keep in touch, in whatever way works for you both. There's no formula for how often or how long. For some of your contacts, it will be a quick e-mail. For others, a periodic breakfast (or any meal, actually). For still others, maintaining contact will take the form of attending an event together, while for others, it will be a phone call. The point is to keep the relationship "warm", so you can call when you need advice or assistance. And make sure the other person knows he or she can do the same.

In my experience, the most successful people are those who take networking seriously and make it a priority. Nobody becomes a success in business by going it alone.

RELATIONSHIP BUILDING

By now you've noticed that I make a distinction between networking and relationship building. Relationship building is networking taken to a higher level. It's when your contact becomes more than a contact; someone with whom you have a personal relationship based on shared experience, trust and values. It's when you start to socialize as friends as well as business associates. Building relationships takes time; it requires really getting to know the person. When it happens, the boundaries between colleague and friend blur. In very practical business terms, a good relationship will ensure that you get an opportunity for every piece of business that comes up – and you also get the opportunity to fix problems as they arise. I can't tell you how many times I've had colleagues say, "I know M really well. We're old friends. He'll certainly agree to meet with us." So my colleague will try to set up a meeting, and not only will that "old friend" not meet with us – he won't even return the call. Radio silence. And my poor colleague will slink away, embarrassed. That's an example of what is *not* a relationship.

True relationships are based on mutuality. If you have a subservient relationship with a person of high rank and spend your time flattering him or her, you're not building a true relationship. If it's all one way, and the person allows you to take him to dinners, the theater and great events and never reciprocates, if he or she never shares information, never asks for or accepts advice, you haven't got a relationship.

Do be realistic. Despite what I've written about CEOs being approachable, it's generally more effective, early on in your career, to focus on your peer level. I always told my teams at PricewaterhouseCoopers that the entry-level lawyer or investment banker of today (or the fellow alumnus from school) is the partner or CEO of tomorrow. Start off networking and building relationships with those you like and respect, and you'll advance in your careers together.

As you progress in your career, it will be easier to move up the chain and reach for relationships at a higher level. This is the time to take the CEO off the pedestal. In my experience, most top people are delighted to be included on a guest list. Stop and think whether hierarchy is a real barrier – or whether your own fear of rejection and unwillingness to try are keeping you from reaching out and up. Remember, leaders are networkers and relationship builders, too, or they wouldn't be where they are; without networking, they wouldn't have access to the business opportunities that they do.

Now, some might say that with all the current headlines about corporate fraud and misdeeds, building relationships should be avoided, lest you risk charges of cronyism, collusion, conspiracy or any of a host of ethical lapses. I couldn't disagree more. I would argue that one reason all these corporate problems could grow to such proportions is that nobody really knew the perpetrators. They were able to isolate themselves. Some of these folks had their agendas mapped in advance and *wanted* to isolate themselves from relationships. But for those who were swept up in temptation, relationships with colleagues and friends who could have raised questions might have changed the course of events considerably.

In a global business setting, I think building relationships is even more important, because a relationship, as opposed to a networking contact, is based on deep trust and sincerity. A good relationship overcomes cultural and language barriers. Keep in mind, however, that there are cultures in which senior people really *are* unapproachable; the cultural values dictate that the hierarchy can't be breached; authority can't be questioned. (As an auditor, I can tell you it made my job a lot harder!) Cultural differences can be an issue in your attempts at networking. But don't let that stop you from trying once you've done your homework.

Now, how do you build relationships that will benefit you both personally and professionally? The first step is to move beyond the realm of business. Find something you have in common and look for an opportunity to share it, and include spouses and/or significant others. Your common interest might be the theater, a particular spectator sport, a concert or just going out for a nice dinner. Whatever it is, doing it together creates an opportunity to get to know someone on a more personal basis and learn about his or her values, family history, likes and dislikes and on and on. As you go, you'll find out other interests and affiliations that you have in common and you can build on these as well. And just as you did when you started networking, you might make notes to help you remember family members' names so you can ask about them later.

Breaking through to a more personal level in a relationship is not an exact science; it's more of an art. It might happen by sharing a personal milestone (preferably a good one, like a wedding). It might happen by helping a son or daughter network for a job or school admission. (Just be clear that you can't secure the placement; you help with referrals and advice.) It might happen by offering support during a stressful time. The true test of a relationship is when you can replace terms like client, partner, colleague and boss with one word that says it all: friend.

5

MENTORING

Delve into the life of a leader a bit, and you'll probably find someone who has had one or more mentors – and who naturally went on to mentor others. Mentors are, in my view, absolutely essential to a person's professional development. Having an impartial somebody to talk to about how best to approach challenges on the job or what's the next step in a career can be invaluable for both young up-and-comers and mature executives alike.

Leaders who want to develop their talent pool and build the next generation of leadership would do well to encourage mentoring. Nor should the leader shrink from personally taking on one or more mentees; doing so will speak louder than any memo to encourage the practice. That said, I must add that a lot of companies have taken a very formal approach to mentoring, actually forcing the process and assigning mentors for each employee. Admirable, perhaps, but not all that effective, in my experience. The best approach is simply to encourage the team to embrace mentoring. At Genesis Park, the professional leadership development program that I initiated at PricewaterhouseCoopers, we made sure that all participants left the program with mentors of their own choosing or a plan to seek one.

The participants in that program came from all over the world, so, in talking to them, I was able to make a small, unscientific study of how much different cultures value mentoring and how they vary. Based on these conversations and my own observations, I'd say Australia and New Zealand rank first among societies that focus on mentoring. Next would come the Americas – both North and South. Parts of Asia are also good; I'll single out Singapore, Malaysia and Thailand. In parts of Asia where age hierarchies are very rigid, young people might hesitate to approach older folks for advice. But because the very nature of mentoring does not violate but reinforces respect for seniority, if the company encourages it, mentoring can flourish in such cultures.

From what I've seen, some European countries don't emphasize mentoring much at all. The top-ranked people tend to come by their positions based on their years of service and, perhaps because of this, they seem less concerned about developing the next generation of leaders. Perhaps this will change with time, as the new generation of transcultural leaders emerges within these companies and countries.

Interestingly, while the value placed on mentoring varies from place to place, when mentoring happens, it's pretty similar no matter what the culture.

Some prospective mentees look for mentors first through groups that promote mentoring, either inside or outside a company. Professional organizations often run mentoring networks. And some companies set up women's mentoring networks or minority networks or other special-interest groups. I've seen all of these kinds of arrangements work very well – and fail horribly. The success of these programs depends on the commitment to them by the leadership and the mentors and mentees. If it's a tick-the-box kind of thing, it will be a waste of time.

As you advance in your career, you will probably seek a mentor from outside the organization, especially if you are in a top leadership position. In my own career, my most recent mentors have been friends and business colleagues outside my company – people with whom I can discuss ideas, talk about problems and concerns, and really get into the nitty-gritty of difficult situations.

Whether the mentoring relationship originates within or outside the company, I believe the responsibility for its success belongs to both the mentor and the mentee. The best mentoring relationships are characterized by several qualities:

- **Connection:** The best mentoring relationships result when there's a basis for the relationship – a connection between the two people. It might be a common professional specialty, but it can arise from a shared hometown or university, an interest in sports or music – something the two people have in common.

- **Mentee initiation:** The process works best when the mentee identifies someone he or she would like to work with and invites that person to be a mentor.

- **No conflict of interest:** It should go without saying that mentees shouldn't report directly to their mentors; if they did, the mentee couldn't seek guidance on how to deal with problems encountered in working with the boss! A mentor–mentee relationship should be independent of an employee–supervisor relationship so that it can give rise to open, honest dialogue without fallout on performance evaluations or salary reviews.

- **Trust:** This quality is more difficult to pin down; it takes time to develop. The mentee should observe the potential mentor long enough to evaluate whether he or she is discreet enough to confide in and secure enough to sincerely have the mentee's best interest in mind.

- **Time:** Both sides need to be willing to devote time and effort to the relationship. Not so much as to be burdensome, but mentor and mentee should be willing to get together at least once each quarter and check in with an occasional phone call or e-mail. And the mentor should be available, within reason, when the mentee has a question that needs a timely answer.

- **Honesty:** Both sides must be honest. The mentor can't be a cheerleader. He or she must be willing to tell it straight, good or bad, and then help craft a solution. By the same token, the mentee must be honest, and if the relationship isn't working, or isn't working anymore, he or she should respectfully and tactfully exit. (A note or a phone call to the effect that, "I really appreciate the time we spent together, but now I think I need to connect with someone whose experience and expertise more closely reflects the issues I'm dealing with, so I am going to look for a female/male mentor with experience in China who likes gardening as much as I do.") (In other words, fill in your own specifications.)

I've had some wonderful mentors over the years and in turn I have mentored many, many bright young people; it's been among the most rewarding aspects of my career. My greatest satisfaction is to see their advancement and success. Some of my closest mentees at PricewaterhouseCoopers are now in top positions there. When I left the firm there was a party in my honor, and I was able to invite many of the mentees I'd worked with over the years. That was priceless.

One surprising aspect of being a mentor is that you might find yourself being reverse-mentored. That is, you can learn quite a lot from the young folks coming up: how they perceive the company, if the relationship is within your firm, and, in general, how they perceive the world. Sometimes a reverse mentor will be the mentee, but in other cases, the relationship will be an informal one. Young people have often said to me, "It's so nice that you spend time with us." I tell them that I learn as much from them as they do from me – and it's true!

6

EXECUTIVE PRESENCE

If you've ever heard phrases like "She really fills a room" or "He commands attention," what you are hearing about is executive presence. When a person with executive presence walks into a room, you notice. When someone like this speaks, you pay attention. You take notes. You remember. You find yourself quoting the person. And you want executive presence, too. The question is: How to develop it?

The answer has many facets, but the good news is that you can consciously cultivate executive presence. And if you start early, by the time you assume a leadership position, the "presence thing" will come naturally. (But take heart, you can catch up later.)

From what I've observed, executive presence, also known as boardroom presence, has three major components:

- **Deportment:** How you conduct yourself is key. By this I don't mean knowing which fork to use at a formal dinner, although there's nothing wrong with that. A leader, however, must exude substance and confidence, must make people feel comfortable with – and proud of – the fact that he or she is their leader. Visible lack of confidence on the part of the leader will not inspire confidence in the team being led.

- **Appearance:** It helps – a lot – if you look the part. This doesn't mean movie-star or model looks. It means being well groomed. It means choosing stylish but appropriate clothing. It means being aware of the image you project. The "starving artist" with shoes worn through, rumpled shirt and wild hair overdue for a cut might make it in the café, but not in most business settings. Likewise, the low-cut blouse and ultrashort skirt, though ubiquitous in the media, are not appropriate in the business world.

- **Humility:** If you are too impressed with yourself, chances are that others will not be. In, fact, they might even think less of you. There's a big different between being confident and throwing your weight around. If you think you've got all the answers and are clearly uninterested in hearing the views of others, the people around you will catch on fast. But if you are a bit understated and self-effacing (without seeming underconfident – a delicate balance), this will reflect favorably on you. If you listen to what people have to say, if you show that you respect others, no matter what their rank, you will likely win them over.

Cultivate these qualities in yourself and you might just hear people whispering the phrase "executive presence" – and realize they're talking about you.

Executive presence is even more important when you venture onto the global scene, where showing respect for the culture you are dealing in is vital. You don't want your manner, appearance or conduct to breach local customs and values – and sink your credibility before you even get started. Here, a keen eye and ear for what is going on around you and sense of what might be called cultural delicacy are invaluable. In some places, the business-casual style of dress will be construed as disrespectful; better to err on the side of a style that is slightly more formal, but not too showy either.

Elsewhere, you'll have to tone down your air of confidence and develop a sense of deference. Too often, in my observation, executives from the United States and the United Kingdom show up somewhere in the world with an attitude that communicates "Let me tell you what you're doing wrong." This never works. On the other hand, if you speak intelligently but not too forcefully, and with substance, your odds of winning respect and accomplishing your goals are pretty high. A British friend of mine took a leadership posting in Germany and, from the start, he carried himself as though he had as much to learn as to teach. He very soon won the respect of his team and his tenure in Germany was successful.

In some parts of Asia, the international balancing act can become even trickier, again because tradition there holds that respect is accorded automatically to senior, titled individuals. Given this cultural tendency, it might seem safe to assume that non-Asians heading up teams there will win respect and loyalty based on title or rank alone. But life isn't quite that tidy; it's much wiser for the outsider to go in prepared to pay his or her respects to the senior people there, and to use the tools of leadership to win the loyalty of the team. As younger people win top positions there, too, the Western model of respect for leaders based on who they are and not on seniority or hierarchy will likely take hold.

Be aware that the perks of high rank can lead you down the path away from executive presence and onto the one marked "LINOs This Way". Executives who revel too much in things like the chauffeur, the prime seating, the private plane and the special attention they can command are in danger of losing focus on what matters. Perks and leadership are not mutually exclusive, by any means. A chauffeured limo or a private plane can be an efficiency measure when an executive's time is more valuable than money – and let's face it, these things are pleasurable as well. It's when these things are flaunted, or when they are used with no consideration for those around the executive – the drivers, the waiters, the ticket takers, the pilots and so on – that executive presence slips away and a spoiled LINO emerges. By contrast, I am always impressed when I see a big-time CEO traveling alone on a plane without an entourage. I'm even more impressed if, when the plane lands, that CEO walks to the baggage claim and stands in line like everybody else and picks up his or her bags without someone in uniform to do the work. Now, there might be a driver waiting outside and, if so, that's great – it's a real time saver. But choosing to wrangle your own bag when you can easily order someone else to do it – that's a form of executive presence, too.

Over the years, I've developed some guidelines for cultivating executive presence in various settings:

- **When interacting with team members:**
  - *Be aware that people – both within and outside the company – are watching you.* You are setting an example, representing the company, leading a team and conducting business all at the same time, and all require executive presence.
  - *Be pleasant and friendly, but not too casual or familiar.* You want to be seen as a serious, substantive, caring leader, not a buddy or a pal.
  - *Do try to engage people on a business and personal level.* Leaders who don't care about their team members' lives outside of work will find themselves losing people. Let them see your personal side and your ability to be human. A bit of self-deprecation can go a long way.

50

- *Keep your language clean.* Don't use off-color language or make remarks that will be offensive to particular groups.
- *Don't air dirty laundry or criticize predecessors or others in the company.*
- *Pay attention to every member of the team and to others within the organization.* Use every interaction as an opportunity to teach, learn, influence or build consensus.
- *Remember that true executive presence is always "on".*

■ **When you join a group for the first time:**
  - *Make a low-key entrance.* Don't jump in too quickly. Remember that most of the others in the group will know each other and the subject matter better than you do. Listen for a while to find out what's going on. That means listening to what's officially on the agenda, and what's happening as subtext. Take some time to "read" the meeting. Identify the leader. Pick out the key players. And understand who your "challenges" will be. The latter are not hard to spot; they're the ones who are either not contributing and don't seem involved, or talking too much without saying anything of substance.
  - *Ask whether there is material you can study to learn more about the subject at hand or the group.* Better yet, see if you can arrange to do this before your first meeting.
  - *When you start to contribute, acknowledge that you might have to play catch-up.* Making a wrong assumption and spouting off on it will set you back. When you enter the conversation, lead with, "I'm not sure if I understood this correctly, but I think I heard…" and then sum up the part of the discussion that you want to refer to before making your point. Make it clear that you are open to clarification if you didn't understand what was being said.

- *Use your experience to offer a different perspective.* For example: "I live in India, and I have witnessed the impact of outsourcing from the point of view of the local people." Or: "I went to school in Buenos Aires, and I worked part-time to support my studies, so I can tell you a bit about how business is transacted there."

Finally, remember that executive presence is not something you put on and take off like an overcoat. It's always part of you. You never know when you're being observed, or whether something you say or do will be repeated to others. That shouldn't scare a true transcultural leader, who has cultivated habits of deportment, appearance and an attitude of respect for others that will create the right impression no matter what the situation. Leaders command attention not because of the rank they hold, but because of what they say and do and how they say and do it.

7

TEAM BUILDING

In recent years, the business world has made the term "team-work" something of a cliché, but sometimes clichés carry a lot of wisdom, and that's the case here. Teamwork is critical to the success of any organization. No single person can achieve the goals of a complex organization alone. That's why building good teams is such a necessary skill for a leader. Whether you are heading up a project, a department, a conference, a division – or an entire multinational corporation – building a strong team is key to your success.

A team that works well is great for what I call "leveraging the organization". By this I mean that when team members really work together and know each other's capabilities, they can tap the strength of the entire company. Being able to say, "I don't know the answer, but I will call my colleague who does," is extremely powerful.

BUILDING TEAMS

The optimal situation is one in which the leader assembles the team and establishes its working culture from scratch. There might be times when a leader must work with a team that has been established by a predecessor. In such cases, it's even more important to establish the right working culture and make sure that the team buys into your approach. Here are what I consider to be the attributes of successful teams:

- **Diversity:** Some people dismiss diversity as a gesture of political correctness. They could not be more wrong. Diversity is an absolute necessity for a team, and when I say diversity, I mean it in every sense of the word: gender, race, religion, nationality, sexual orientation, culture, personality type, area of expertise. Over the years, I've noticed that diverse teams are more successful than homogeneous ones – and, by the way, more fun. I've worked on teams that were not diverse – the old-fashioned, white-male-dominated kind – and they were never as good as the diverse teams. In my view, the more homogeneous the team and the more the members are alike in background and values, the more the team is likely to resist challenging conventional thinking. For whatever reason, the homogeneous teams also tend to be more political, and their members generally seem more eager to "kiss up" to the boss. It's a cycle that feeds on itself: the homogeneous teams are usually selected by LINOs who don't want to be challenged. And they get what they ordered. As a result, not much happens.

  In the international marketplace, a diverse team is a must. In this kind of environment, creating a team with a global, or worldly, point of view is imperative. And I'm not talking about team members who have traveled and racked up air miles; I am referring to people who bring different cultural perspectives to the team, who understand that they will encounter cultural differences and who will be sensitive to those differences. In practical terms, diversity can also be a selling point in the international marketplace. I can recall several cases in which homogeneous teams were introduced to clients and, in each case, the client looked up and down the table and rejected the whole team before anybody got to say a word. The explanation was always something like, "If this is your team, it won't work for us. We are a diverse organization, with women and people of color from all parts of the world. We can't select a vendor whose team is not as diverse as we are." This reaction usually sends the LINO scrambling for a quick solution – that is, a few faces to broaden the spectrum – but this can't compare with carefully selecting the right people for the team, right from the start.

One caveat: sometimes a diverse team – any team, really – takes time to gel. An INSEAD alumna recently told me about her MBA team. (At INSEAD, MBA candidates are grouped into five-person teams during the first four months of the program.) Her team consisted of a Russian diplomat, an Israeli fighter pilot, a French engineer, a Canadian entrepreneur and herself (a member of a Japanese financial firm). For the first month, they couldn't stand each other, she said. Soon enough, though, it dawned on them that they all had something to learn from every member of the group. From that point on, they got along, and their team became a productive one. This is so important – the realization that we all have so much to learn from others, particularly those whose experience and perspective differ from our own.

Now, some executives will swear that implementing a strategy of diversity is a major challenge. They say that to get the best people, they need to go with proven talent, and if all that talent happens to be white, Anglo-Saxon and male, so be it. I reject this argument. If you go with the talent you know, you will wind up with more of what you've got. This is not to say that white male Anglo-Saxons should be excluded from consideration (I would have been excluded along with the rest!), but, rather, that they should be part of a broader pool of candidates. When I build teams, I always call for more than one candidate for each position, and I insist on diversity among the candidates. The "diverse" candidate doesn't always get the job, but enough of them do, and those who don't are invariably considered for other opportunities. Those who are chosen then move on to other positions … and suddenly the talent pool is a lot more diverse than it was before. You just have to start the ball rolling.

- **Responsibility:** Teams are most successful when the leader makes a clear delineation of roles and responsibilities. When building a team, the worst thing a leader can do is be ambiguous about either of these items. The team's organizational chart can be a major point of contention. I've seen LINOs who can't, for whatever reason, institute reporting lines. Instead of telling a team member simply, "You will report to E on this project," the LINO winks and says, "Don't worry about the organizational chart; you really report to me." Not only does this undermine E, who is supposed to be in charge; it is destabilizing to the whole team, and brings on confusion, political chaos and worse. Smart leaders make sure that the people they empower are truly empowered – and that everyone else on the team knows it. This is particularly important with multicultural teams, in which, to use just one example, some members might automatically assume a male team member is in charge because that's the custom. In such cases, it's wise for the transcultural leader to spend time publicly in the company of the "surprise" choice, so that everyone knows that the reporting lines are real. Leaders must set their people up for success.

Delegating responsibility is another key technique in building a good team. When you delegate, you not only spell out what must be done, but you also make the team accountable for the results. Some LINOs are uncomfortable with delegating, and wind up micromanaging the work of the team, doing all the "important work" and delegating only the menial stuff (and questioning even that). Failure to delegate can be demoralizing to individuals who are supposed to be managing particular tasks and to the team as a whole. I like to give people what I think they can handle. If they prove they can do the job, I give them more or position them for more responsibility elsewhere in the organization.

- **Inclusiveness:** I once worked with a leader who knew everyone in the organization, or seemed to. When we walked through the cafeteria, everyone would know his name and say hello. His secret: He paid attention to the whole team, not just the professional staff, but the support team as well. He made everybody feel important. I vowed to emulate him and have done my best to do so. I believe that in order for a team to function at its best, everyone has to feel important. That comes when the leader pays attention to the whole team.

- **Politics:** One of my least favorite words. But politics is present everywhere. The leader – as well as the aspiring leader – need not become a master politician, but he or she must be aware of the organization's political culture and figure out how to navigate it. Your primary navigating tools are transparency, honesty and confidence in your own values. I think it's possible to succeed in most organizations by being politically aware, but not driven by politics; that is, not letting politics dictate your behavior. Here's an example: I once faced a situation in which two of my superiors wanted me to do separate projects for them. The timing was such that I simply couldn't do both. At that moment, the two were locked into a power struggle and the situation threatened to become ugly. My solution was to be straight with both players and tell them I'd be happy to work with either, but that I couldn't do both jobs in the time allotted. I said my piece and was pleased that I had made them responsible for resolving their political turf battle without getting sucked into it. But in the face of my wonderfully sensible approach, neither would budge. Politics prevailed. Finally, their boss had to intervene. He called me into his office and asked me two questions: What did I want to do? And what would be best for the firm? Fortunately, I had a single answer for both questions. One of the parties to this struggle was in it just for the battle; he really didn't need me for continuity's sake, as he claimed. So, choosing my words carefully, I told the boss that. He agreed with me, assigned me to the other project and proceeded to let the "politician" know that he was not pleased. It was a great lesson in how not to fight for what you don't need just to score political points. (On the other hand, I was lucky to have a wise boss. I've heard stories of LINOs who actually promote political competition on the misguided theory that it's good for productivity. In my view, this is a disastrous strategy. If the big boss had not been so wise about my warring superiors, I would have, once again, learned something important about my workplace and done some thinking about my long-range plan.)

Let's look at another example. Some years ago, I was working with a multinational client that that had a significant operation in Venezuela. The head of our local team there had alienated the client and my boss called me into his office and said, "Go down there and fix it." Immediately the alarm bells in my head began to ring. I knew that if I went to Caracas and simply tried to take over, I would face the ire of the local man and possibly that of his staff – and they might well try to undermine my efforts. But if I didn't try to undo the damage he had done, the client might lose patience and seek another solution. I suppose one option might have been to decline the assignment and make up an excuse for not traveling to Venezuela. Instead, following my own rules of honesty, transparency and sticking to my own values (in this case, not becoming embroiled in politics), I explained my concerns to my boss and said, "Decide on your objective before you send me to the wolves. You and I need to agree on what defines success in this situation." The boss thought a bit and told me he wanted to finish the audit and salvage as much of our client relationship as we could without totally alienating the local office – and I went to Venezuela. I knew I couldn't go in like a rescuer on horseback. I decided to simultaneously engage the head of the local team and keep him far away from the client. At our first meeting I informed him that, considering the situation, I would become the point man for client contact, but would rely heavily on him for guidance. I met with him daily and took him out to dinner several times to "discuss" the project. Meanwhile, I met with the client and worked with the rest of our staff to get the project done. I traveled back and forth between Venezuela and New York for several months. In the end, our local chief did not lose face, the staff did not revolt, the client was happy, my boss was happy and I had navigated a very political situation without resorting to the kind of political behavior I so detested.

MANAGING TEAMS

So far, I've covered the principles of building and dealing with teams. Now, for some practical advice on managing them:

- **Checking in:** As I've written earlier, a leader can't assume that no news is good news. It's imperative to stay in touch with the team during the course of a project. Checking in can take the form of phone calls, memos and other written communications; conversations with individual team members; or meetings. Lots of people dislike meetings, but a team really can't do without them. Whether you meet in person or via teleconference (or both if logistics and geography dictate), teams have to get together periodically to make sure things are progressing according to plan. And there's nothing like the immediacy of a conversation to see how the work is going. If it appears that the team is moving off course, the leader must be prepared to take action – to communicate any concerns to the team directly, review the project objectives with them and make a plan to get back on track.

- **Managing meetings:** Managing teams at meetings is critical, because it's here that the team members meet in force to exchange their news and views. So you need to foster a meeting culture in which people are engaged, prepared, ready to share and expect to be productive.
  - *Set an agenda and stick to it.* The point of the meeting is to get progress reports from the team, share information

and make decisions that will enable all to proceed with their work. An agenda will help keep you on track.

- *Set a time limit and stick to it.* Time is a valuable commodity for everyone, and often people have to travel to attend a meeting. If you respect your team's needs and they feel confident that they can make that plane or get to that dinner, they'll be better able to focus on business.
- *Make sure everyone is focused on the meeting.* No side conversations, no e-mails. I prohibit open computers during meetings. All team members must be "totally present" and involved in the session.
- *Invite only those whose presence is required.* I used to see people bring whole armies of assistants just in case they were asked a question they couldn't answer. The atmosphere was totally counterproductive and distracting. The leader should make it clear that it's okay to say, "I'm not sure, but I'll find out and disseminate the information as soon as possible."
- *Make decisions.* There's nothing worse than sitting in a meeting all day and not coming to closure.

What I find with these rules is that people are more respectful of the occasion and of each other, are more prepared, and they tend to finish business more quickly and productively. They also tend to participate in the discussion and give their points of view more actively, which is exactly what a leader should be aiming for; it's important not just for the input and the diversity of views presented (which, as I've said, is crucial), but because it helps to build a better, more cohesive team.

- **Following up:** When a decision is made, whether in a meeting or otherwise, it's important to follow up and let the team know what has been decided and what the next steps are. In the age of e-mail, this has become almost effortless. With a few keystrokes, everyone has received your message. If the decision was made at a meeting, your follow-up will be a memory jogger and "clarifier" that ensures that everyone is on the same page (and it will bring any absentees up to speed). In addition to following up after meetings and other decision-making occasions, it's important to give periodic updates and ask for regular feedback.

- **Evaluating the team's efforts:** Successful teams depend on constructive feedback from their leaders. I've heard countless tales of the team member who feels lost and hasn't a clue as to how the work is going because the LINO in charge of the team has not taken the time to give feedback. Feedback can be a tricky business, but honesty is the best policy. If something is wrong, say so. If something is going well, offer praise.

  - *Positive feedback:* Make your praise immediate and make it public. A rewards system that recognizes teamwork can likewise be a powerful motivator in creating a team environment that is collegial and cooperative. Financial incentives are always appreciated, but any kind of reward for a job well done – company awards, employee-of-the-month designations, group outings – can be just as effective.

  - *Negative feedback:* Keep in mind that every team will have its stars and its underperformers. The stars are easy; it's the underperformers who need the most management. In addition to feedback, it's important to give them roles they can handle, and keep them from dragging down the performance of the rest of the team. Of course, negative feedback should always be delivered privately and in a professional manner, and it goes without saying that it should not become a personal attack. The emerging field of coaching holds that people will receive criticism better if you first point out something good about their performance. If this style of feedback suits you, by all means use it.

- *Feedback for a multicultural team:* With a globally diverse team, it's wise to avoid rushing in with a feedback format that worked in the home office without evaluating how it will be received in a particular culture. For example, some companies have adopted the "360" form, so called because the individual's performance is reviewed from a 360-degree perspective – by superiors, peers and those in junior positions as well. The 360 works best with teams that have been assembled in a corporate culture of mutual respect and collegiality, not those rife with political rivalries. But, here's the catch for the globally diverse team: I would not institute a 360 in cases where the team members come from cultures that revere seniority and hierarchy, as the junior people will hesitate to criticize their bosses. You can find other formats that deliver your message. In the end, the main thing is to give feedback often during a project. Silence is never the answer.

- **Resolving conflicts:** Sometimes team members will find themselves at odds with one another. They're human beings, after all, and conflict happens. The cause might be a difference over the team's work. Or it might be one person's behavior: a case of "bad blood" or past history, or just a personality conflict. Perhaps it will arise from a cultural difference. Whatever the reason, conflict is something a leader must deal with directly and quickly. My approach has always been to get those involved into a room together and hash it out. I start by offering my assessment of what is wrong and then I ask them to each give their side. In most cases, this simple discussion creates a ground for resolution. Often the leader's most difficult task in resolving conflicts in this way is to get the "combatants" together. Once, I arranged a dinner for a pair of team members who were not working well, without telling either that the other was coming. I reserved a private room with no windows, arrived early and greeted the first guest. The second arrived shortly afterward. Because our space was private, I had the element of surprise in my favor – and they *were* surprised! I did the talking at first and told them how much I respected both of them and how much they contributed to the organization. I said that I thought we would all be much better off if they could find a way to work together. We wound up having a nice meal and a good conversation. I can't say that they ever became friends, but at least we reached a point of effective détente. And for you, as leader, that's a successful outcome. Your team members still might not like each other, but they should know they have to clear the air and work together. (And sometimes they'll surprise you by becoming best buddies.)

- **Dealing with bad behavior:** When someone shows a lack of respect for others, makes a discriminatory remark, shows cultural insensitivity or indulges in other antisocial behavior, the leader must act. He or she must let it be known that such actions will not be tolerated. I have probably ticked some people off in my day, but when people misbehave, I call them on it – in private, but directly and firmly. If the bad behavior happens in a meeting, I pull the offender aside as soon as possible and make my feelings known. Once, a British colleague was leading a discussion at a meeting of about 20 people from around the world – but he wasn't really leading, he was dominating! No one could get a word in edgewise. Anglo-Saxon cultures – British and Americans alike – sometimes have a tendency to take the floor and hold it; it's a cultural trait that a transcultural leader must guard against. I called for a break (something a bit uncharacteristic for me) and asked him, "How do you think it's going? He replied enthusiastically, "Great. We'll be done with this early!" I replied bluntly: "That's because you have basically railroaded everyone in the room!" He was shocked. He hadn't realized what he had been doing. To his credit, when we reconvened he was a changed man, and from then on, the session had all the give-and-take I could have hoped for.

- **Fun:** I believe that the most productive teams are those who can get along with one another and have fun together. This can be as simple as a good-natured discussion during meetings and other encounters, or it can take the form of a meal or event where the team comes together. It doesn't have to cost a lot of money, but it should be something that everyone on the team can participate in and enjoy. I remember one time when a team rented out a billiard hall for dinner. The team members relaxed and enjoyed each other's company. It was probably the least expensive, most enjoyable event we ever had.

Assembling and nurturing – and I do mean nurturing – a team is some of the hardest work a leader will ever do. Failure to do it, however, carries with it the risk of having a team that is not cohesive, doesn't work effectively and can't deliver the excellent product that your clients demand. I owe some of my most rewarding work experiences to teams of talented individuals who were exciting to work with and share with. A good team turns work into pleasure.

8

SETTING GOALS

Setting goals sounds simple. You decide what you want to accomplish and then go about doing it. But the reality is much more complex and can reveal a great deal about the kind of leader (or LINO) who is in charge. Some opt to under-promise and overdeliver. Some choose to avoid commitment to any goal at all. Some go through the motions of setting goals that sound terrific, but then you realize that you can't quite pin down what they're trying to achieve or how to measure their progress. I don't have a lot of patience for any of these goal-setting styles. I believe that the best leaders set aggressive, yet achievable goals and then work with their teams to meet them.

When I say "aggressive goals", I'm not referring to hostile takeovers or other such scenarios. I mean setting high goals – increasing revenues by a whopping percentage or getting a deal done by a seemingly impossible date. The typical LINO will set a safe goal, say, of increasing revenues by 5 per cent, even though he knows his team can comfortably manage 10 per cent. I'd rather fall a bit short of an aggressive goal than beat a safe, low one. I might set an aggressive goal of a 15 per cent increase, knowing that in all likelihood the team can reach 13 per cent with a little sweat – and that they might just hit 15!

In 2002, I was asked by PricewaterhouseCoopers to sell its consulting division, PricewaterhouseCoopers Consulting.

It had been a robust US$5 billion business before 2000, but in that year, for a variety of reasons, the market began to pressure the Big Five accounting firms to get out of the consulting business. Our firm reacted with an announcement that the division was for sale, but then... nothing happened. And the business went downhill. When I was asked to step in, the division had been on the market for nearly two years. The team working on the project – some 30 people from within the firm, as well as outside lawyers and investment bankers – was by then rather demoralized. They had lost faith in their assignment. After studying the situation, I decided that the way to make the sale was to commit to an aggressive goal – and to do so in public. When I first floated my idea, some team members were skeptical; interestingly, they divided along cultural lines, with the Europeans characteristically risk-averse. Many European partners asked me, "Do we really have to do this?" Of course, the answer was yes, and I took pains to reassure them as I explained why it had to be. And on 1 February 2002, we announced that we would file for an IPO within 90 days. The business world took note, and the team was energized – even my reluctant European friends. The publicity generated by the announcement didn't hurt either. As it turned out, the team was ready for a major push. They knew that one way or another, they would be done with this phase of the plan in 90 days. After two years of being in limbo, that was a relief. I was proud but not surprised when they met the goal. It actually took 91 days, but nobody complained. The filing took place in May, and the consulting division was sold to IBM in July.

It might sound like I took a big risk in setting a 90-day deadline for such a labor-intensive filing, but I assure you that I didn't. I had done my homework and I knew the team could pull it off. And that is the secret to setting aggressive goals: Always base the goal on a realistic assessment of what can be done. A good leader will resist the temptation to make up a goal based on visions of glory for leader and team. Set ego aside, roll up your sleeves and get to work. I've broken the process down into a series of steps:

- **Do your due diligence:** Your goal must be rest on your careful and honest assessment of what is possible, with a good measure of confidence and optimism stirred into the recipe.
  - *Start by getting the facts.* Use sources both from within and outside the organization.
  - *Identify all the potential outcomes.* Rank each in order of preference from 1 through 5.
  - *List the events that would have to take place and the support you will need to achieve the top-ranked outcomes.*
  - *Consult with the team that will be responsible for implementing the plan, as well as your superiors and your mentors to get all their opinions.*
  - *Based on all of this, you can zero in on the optimal, achievable goal.* Map out a plan to make it happen.

- **Enlist your team:** You've already consulted with the team on how they view the situation. Once you have decided which route to take, getting the team to buy into it is absolutely critical. This might involve traveling to meet with team members in far corners of the world, one to one and in groups, or it might take the form of phone calls, teleconferences – you name it. All the while, you must be sensitive to cultural issues that might arise in response to your stated goal. Listen to team members' concerns. If they balk, ask for alternatives and work through the potential outcomes with them. If you still feel your goal is sound, say so. At this point, the team will generally join forces and move heaven and earth to get the job done. Keep in mind that getting to the buy-in point can be tougher than actually meeting your aggressive goal. Everyone must have a chance to speak, and adequate discussion and consultation must take place. The leader must factor this step into the process; it can't be skipped if you want optimum team performance. (Occasionally you will encounter hold-outs who, for various reasons, can't buy in. This is the time to exert the power of your position and inform them, publicly and privately, that your decision will stand. If you have previously worked to gain their trust, as good leaders do, they'll support you because they know you have listened to them, you are still listening and that if your thinking proves to be flawed you will revisit your decision with them.)

- **Communicate with your superiors:** Even your bosses might wonder if your goal is too aggressive. Just as you did with the team, you must share your due diligence findings with upper management and obtain a buy-in. You'll need their full support to meet your goal.

- **Announce your decision:** Based on all of this, set the goal and announce it publicly. You're on the record – an excellent motivator.

- **Set up checkpoints along the way:** Regular interaction with key team members and the team as a whole is vital if the leader is to be apprised of any challenges that come up. And with regular check-ins, the team knows the leader is available to help overcome them.

I honestly can't remember a major goal that I set using these guidelines that my teams did not meet or exceed. Now, there might be times when circumstances intervene, when world events, economic news, scientific breakthroughs – all sorts of situations that you can't have foreseen – suddenly emerge to interfere with your goal. With a good communication system in place, you and your team can identify whatever comes up, and change tactics as necessary. And those instances will be rare. If your due diligence has been thorough, most of the time, your goal will stand. I'm convinced that if more organizations set aggressive but achievable goals, productivity would soar.

DECISION MAKING

Making decisions and setting goals have a lot in common – for both, you've got to do due diligence, elicit buy-in from your team and superiors, act with confidence and so on. One could argue that setting goals is a form of decision making; I could almost have covered both in one chapter. But decision making is much broader in scope. In this section, I'd like to address how the leader can develop a sense and a style of decision making.

There's a joke that in the United States that the dominant decision-making style is "Ready, fire, aim!" In Europe, the dominant style is "Ready, aim, aim, aim, aim … ." This always gets chuckles, but there's a lot of truth to it. Americans do tend to be pretty quick on the trigger when making decisions. And Europeans tend to take their time before they decide which way to go. I believe that either extreme can be costly. Decide too fast, without enough information or consultation, and you can decide yourself into disaster. Take too much time to make up your mind and you can get so bogged down that you get stuck right where you are.

I tell this joke when I talk to students about the importance of decision making to good leadership. I've seen a lot in my years in business, and I've concluded that a huge proportion of the problems that arise relate in some way to lack of decisiveness by those in charge. Too often, LINOs are "managed" by the politically savvy under them, who are invariably striving to maintain the status quo and preserve their positions. They set up roadblocks to decision and action.

The good news is that there are plenty of organizations whose leaders make their decisions effectively and wisely. I was impressed by the decision making of our advisory team in South Africa when they were faced with the postapartheid challenge of bringing people of color onto their local management team. The changes they made were fast, substantive and seamless. When I attended a leadership meeting in Cape Town in 2004, I was pleased to see how well the newly constituted team had come together.

SUBSTANCE

A good leader will make decisions based, not on self-preservation and not on pressure from the politicians who fester in the organization, but on *what the best course of action is for the organization and its stakeholders.* That's what I mean when I refer to the substance, or sense, underlying a decision. Now, there are many LINOs out there who seem to be master decision makers; when in truth, they have only mastered the style part of the equation at the expense of substance. A true leader must master both.

As an example, a LINO will typically point to the performance of the company's stock as proof that a decision has been made in the best interest of the organization. Indeed, it's become quite fashionable to use share price as a measure of what's good for the organization. In the United States, for example, top managers of publicly held companies have a fiduciary responsibility to put their shareholders first. But that bit of legalese doesn't go deep enough. When the LINOs say, "Our first duty is to the shareholders," are they talking about all shareholders? Or the long-term shareholders? And how about the employee-shareholders who have both their savings and their current and future income tied up in the company? The world saw what happened to the employee-shareholders of Enron, how they lost their jobs as well as their retirement savings based on the decisions of that firm's so-called leaders, even though the company's performance in the quarters leading up to the debacle had been good. And beyond the shareholders, what of the other constituents? These can include government regulators, consumers, the community where you're doing business and/or the environment. A decision that affects any of them can spill over to soil the company's image – which might, in turn, affect share price! Each decision will affect a chain of stakeholders, and the make-up of the chain will differ from case to case. The wise leader will identify the stakeholders who are pertinent to each decision and consider them along with share price.

Of course, there are times when share price should be a factor in a leader's decision. Too often, though, it is a short-term fix made at the expense of the long-term picture. True leaders, I believe, make their decisions with both the present and the future in mind, with tactics for the short term and strategies for the long term. Sometimes a negative short-term performance is required to bring about the positive long-term result. Too few organizations are brave enough to tell the market or their shareholders that they are making a short-term sacrifice for a long-term gain. But this is precisely the kind of decision a leader might have to make to ensure the health of the organization.

Consider these decision-making principles in light of some of the colossal business failures of the past several years.

Study the Enrons, Worldcoms and Parmalats and you will find – besides the charges of greed and dishonesty that have been aimed at those responsible – a basic failure in decision making early on in the game. All fraud starts somewhere, usually with a small decision. In most of these cases, the decision in question was motivated by short-term profit. Whether it was at the top or halfway down the chain of command, somebody had to *decide* not to do the right thing. And one bad decision led to another and another. This is why I say the substance of a decision is so crucial.

My formula for decision making is much the same as for goal setting:

- **First, due diligence and consultation:** Get the facts, and consider the stakeholders and the good of the organization. Get input both internally and externally. This applies whether you are setting a goal, deciding on a strategy, acquiring a business, making a key hire or any of the myriad decisions a leader will face. Some period of gathering opinions and including the team is critical. The amount of time you spend on this will be determined by the situation at hand and the urgency of the decision. You can't spend three weeks getting input when the seller needs an answer tomorrow. Keep in mind that the nature and extent of consultation will vary from culture to culture. Many societies are quite formal and require that certain hierarchies be respected and that consultation take place within the hierarchy. This can be a bit tedious, especially to those weaned on the fast-paced American style of decision making, but in my experience it is certainly important. The bottom line: be aware of differences and make sure to ask about local customs before you plunge ahead with what works in your own backyard.

- **Analyze the options:** Your analysis can be as simple as a pro and con list on a piece of paper or as complicated as a series of spreadsheets. Work through all possible outcomes, rank them in order of preference – and don't forget to include the ramifications of not taking action.

- **Make your decision:** If the analysis and advice you've received are consistent and compelling, go with them! These are the easy decisions to make (even if they are big ones). They're also easy to communicate and defend. If, however, the analysis and the advice diverge (as is often the case), I go to my closest, most trusted team (internal and external), listen to what they have to say and then make my best decision. (In other words, do the homework and then go with your gut.)

STYLE

Once your decision is made, the way you communicate it and defend it will be a big part of its success:

- **Stand by your decision:** This is key to success. Unless there is compelling evidence that you have made a mistake (more on this below), it's critical that you stand by your decision publicly. I say publicly, because in these media-happy times, you might also have to defend your decision to the press and, by extension, to the world. Not every decision you make will be subject to this level of scrutiny, but some doubtless will, and you should be prepared. Know that defending your decision can be challenging, especially as some in the media seem to revel in creating a game show atmosphere in lieu of serious discussion. Your task is doubly hard if the message you bring is not an easy or popular one (if, for example, as described above, you're making a short-term sacrifice for a long-term gain). But I believe a leader who is honest, open and confident can navigate these tests and come out the victor. (Having a good handle on executive presence helps here, too.)

- **Fire up the team:** It's just as important, if not more so, to defend your decision to your team. First of all, make sure the team coalesces around the decision. I always tell my teams that we can have as much debate and disagreement as they need inside the conference room, but when the decision is made, *everyone* is on board. There's no room for naysayers; they'll destabilize the enterprise. As I said in the chapter on goal setting, if you've done your work as a leader, even the doubters will trust you and work hard toward implementing whatever decision you've made. But getting buy-in is only the first step. You must continue to express your belief in the task at hand and the team's ability to accomplish it. The belief and passion of a leader can inspire a team to great things.

- **Change course when necessary:** In those cases when it appears that you have made the wrong move, or when circumstances force you to reconsider, the best course is honesty. No one can expect a leader to be right 100 per cent of the time, but they do expect that leader to be honest and recognize mistakes. In such cases it is imperative that you chart a new course as quickly as possible, again employing the principles of substance and style to revise and then defend your decision.

I should emphasize here that fear of being wrong is among the worst traits a leader can have. There will always be critics

of every decision you take. The person you have to fire or demote will never be your fan, but leaving someone in place wh⸳⸳⸳ ⸳ doing the job will cost you in productivity and in res⸳ ⸳⸳ ⸳f the team. American readers of this bo⸳ ⸳⸳day-morning quarter-ba⸳ ⸳⸳w of crit-ic ⸳ game.
A ⸳ quar-⸳ nly
⸳ er
⸳

⸳,
⸳n
⸳e
⸳⸳⸳ ⸳ut-
comes of var⸳⸳⸳ ⸳em
with style (confidence, pa⸳⸳⸳ ⸳ally
and externally). And then be prepared ⸳⸳ ⸳ the
next time.

PART III

MILESTONES OF TRANSCULTURAL LEADERS

Your phone rings. Your handheld device beeps to signal a message. A colleague peeks into your office with a "Got a minute?" It could be a routine question and it could be something that will turn your world upside down.

As a transcultural leader, you must be ready for anything. It's not enough to master the techniques and practices of transcultural leadership; you must also think about how to apply them in response to different situations. Of course, you can't predict what the world – or the express delivery service – will bring each day. But there are some kinds of situations that you can anticipate. And you can use the transcultural leadership tools you've cultivated to deal with them.

10

LEADING INTO CHANGE AND INNOVATION

How a leader confronts the concepts of change and innovation can mean the very survival of his or her organization. Does that sound overly dramatic? Here's a story to illustrate my point. Early on in my auditing career, in the mid-1980s, I worked with a leading maker of over-the-counter cold remedies and other consumer products. The company was publicly traded, but the founding family, a major stockholder, was very active and the CEO was a member of the family. The firm had a terrific line-up of brands and a very strong international distribution network, and everything should have been rosy. But I had been their external auditor for about four years when I started to hear the same worried comment over and over from different departments: The company hadn't launched a new product in quite a while. The joke was that the research labs were coming up with new cough drop flavors, but no new products.

So even though the company was quite profitable, it was not growing very fast. Competitors who coveted the company's brands took note. After a hostile takeover attempt and a bidding war between rival corporations, the company was acquired by a competitor. When the CEO addressed the board at its final meeting, he apologized for letting them down. He added that they had also let down his late grandfather, the company founder, who had always said the one thing he wanted his heirs to do was "Build an enduring enterprise".

"We have failed him," the CEO said.

And then he sat down. There was hardly a dry eye in the house.

For me, the moral of this story can be summed up in a wonderfully pithy remark by General Eric Shineski, retired Chief of Staff of the US Army: "If you don't like change, you're going to like irrelevance even less." In the case of my client, irrelevance – to coin a phrase – happened. The company operated from a strategy of preservation rather than growth. It was insular and conservative. When the competition came knocking on the door, management was taken by surprise. If they had been more action-oriented, more aggressive about investing in and developing new products, more aware of the competition and the world at large, they might not have been forced to sell when they did – or at least they might have had more control over the situation.

In the business world, as in politics, science, the arts, technology – pretty much everywhere – change and innovation are twin imperatives. The two concepts – change and innovation – are similar, but they are not the same, and the leader must understand the difference between them and how each relates to the organization. Stated simply, an organization needs regular change to make sure that its products, processes and customer service are best in class, and that they exceed, or at least equal, what the competition has to offer. To stay on top of these issues, you've got to upgrade (read change) often – even if what you're doing is already very good. If you don't change, somebody else will – and suddenly the definition of "very good" will change, too. Likewise, an organization needs to innovate. Periodically, you've got to go beyond routine changes and upgrades and introduce something completely new and different to your market. If your organization is to achieve longevity, innovation must be part of your long-term strategy.

But change and innovation don't just happen. It's up to the leader to create a working culture in which change and innovation are as natural as breathing. And as with so many things, when you are working in a multicultural environment, encouraging a change-and-innovation-oriented culture can be a challenge. Different cultures react to change in different ways. Like people, some thrive on it, while others resist. Their resistance can be traced to a variety of sources. In some cases, the locals don't like taking orders from outsiders. In others, it's because calling attention to oneself is deemed impolite. In still others, it's fear of failure – or fear of success and the tidal wave of more change and innovation that will follow – that stops them. The transcultural leader will identify and address these cultural barriers to change and innovation – and by "address", I don't mean with a show of authority, but with patience and sensitivity.

From what I have observed, of the nations that actively seek a role in the international marketplace, the Anglo cultures are the most change-oriented, followed by South America, much of Asia and spots like South Africa and the United Arab Emirates. The least change-oriented are Continental Europe and Japan. Years ago, I had an idea for a new service that I wanted all of our offices around the globe to start offering. When I unveiled the idea in Japan, it wasn't received warmly, to say the least. I knew from experience that my Japanese colleagues, able though they were, didn't like to be told how to go about their business. So I decided to take a low-key approach. My aim wasn't to force them to add the service; then they wouldn't have sold it enthusiastically in my absence. Instead, I wanted them to buy in, to accept it as the good idea it was. I made four more trips to the Tokyo office and presented the idea each time. Each time I got a frosty reception. Then, on my fifth trip, the managing partner of the office came to me and said, "We have a great idea for a new service." What was it? The same idea I had been pushing for months, of course! But now they were ready to embrace it as their own. So I praised their brilliant idea. I knew they wouldn't attribute it to me, but I didn't care. My own boss knew I had originated it, and what mattered was that the Tokyo office had bought in.

It takes patience (and on occasion, multiple trips halfway around the world), but nurturing a change-and-innovation-oriented culture is one of the most important things a transcultural leader can do to ensure the future of the organization. Here are several key ingredients:

- **Attitude:** The leader must personally embrace change and innovation as part of "business as usual". That applies both in the abstract and to specific ideas. If he or she seems lukewarm about a project, or marginalizes a program as "G's idea", the team will see no reason to embrace individual initiatives or adopt the culture of change and innovation.

- **Latitude:** The leader must allow for failure. Not all ideas will work; in fact, most won't. The statisticians tell us that new products typically fail at a rate of 90 per cent. The leader must therefore create an environment in which team members are secure enough to share their ideas. You can't punish somebody for an innovative idea that doesn't work, or nobody will dare to present an idea. I'm not talking about celebrating failure, but about celebrating and supporting effort and using a failed idea as a learning experience to increase the chances of success the next time.

■ **Resources:** Time and money make things happen. LINOs typically say they want change and/or innovation, but then don't allocate the necessary resources. They pay lip service to the right ideas but leave their teams unsupported and take no responsibility when the idea fails to material- ize. Now, some leaders truly want to foster change and innovation, but lack adequate budgets and staff to under- write a full-fledged R&D program. My advice here is to make a start, by identifying and prioritizing the things that will have the most impact for the smallest investment. A small success now will likely yield more resources in the future. You can also create an "innovation program" and rotate people into and out of it. And remember to give your team "latitude" when it comes to resources. The money and time you spend on a failed idea will seem to have been wasted, but look at it this way: those resources might not bring immediate returns, but they encourage team members to keep on trying.

■ **Training:** Training could well be classified under resources, but the leader's role is essential here, so I've made it a cat- egory on its own. Committing the resources for ongoing training will make change and innovation much easier; with proper training, the team can, when necessary, change its behavior and ways of working, and master new tech- nologies and tools that will result in innovation. Beyond providing the resources, I believe that the leader must set a good example and take part in the training like every- body else – they can't simply encourage others in pursuit of training. The leader must show up for training sessions, get involved and, in doing so, indicate the importance of training and education to the organization. LINOs don't realize how profoundly their own behavior – their simple presence at a training session – can motivate others.

There are many ways to stimulate change and innovation. One way is to be sure that you are keeping up with what's happening with your competition, your market, your clients and the world. You can't develop deep, technical knowledge of every trend, but I like to say that the leader needs to "know just enough to be dangerous" – that is, to know what questions to ask and whom to ask them of. If you don't have at least this much knowledge, you're at the mercy of the market and those developing the product or service. One way to keep in touch is to attend seminars, industry conferences and meetings. Another is to set up a think tank within the organization; put some creative people together and see what they come up with.

Transcultural leaders will take pains to avoid the common mistake of assuming that you only have to keep up with best practices in what used to be called the "developed" world. This isn't true; you really need to keep up with all markets. (Brazilian businesses, for example, are wonderful at putting together commercial "road shows". They'll assemble a group of people with various skills and sponsor them on a tour of various cities around the world to learn best practices and to share their own capabilities.)

CHANGE

An organization where change takes place frequently and organically is generally a healthy organization. As a leader, you can cultivate a culture of change by using your expertise in your field as well as some of the same practices and techniques discussed earlier in this book:

- **Be aware of your competition and the marketplace** as you develop your upgrades and improvements.

- **Use your communication skills** to help the team understand that if the organization does not constantly change and improve, it will fall behind. As always, let them express their concerns and feelings about change.

- **Be open and transparent** about the need for change and about what's taking place. Some leaders are afraid to even mention the word "change" for fear that it will upset the team, but my view is that we have to be honest and transparent about it, and turn it into an acceptable and expected situation.

- **Reward those who contribute** to the culture of change, who come up with ideas and/or implement change programs successfully. (And never penalize the ones who try hard but don't quite make it.)

That said, beware of change for the sake of change. Change must be meaningful; I've seen many organizations go to fantastic lengths to do something differently, just to be perceived as doing *something*. But does that something add value? Just think back to the go-go years of mergers and acquisitions and you'll find examples that go both ways; some of those deals did add value, but many did not. At the time, however, the CEOs and other high-ranking people responsible for those deals reaped handsome rewards. (And no-value, change-for-change's-sake deals have been at the root of many of the business scandals of the recent past, such as Enron and Worldcom.)

Sometimes people talk about "change fatigue" – the stress that can accompany change within an organization. Market forces might dictate that change (and/or innovation) will come more often and in bigger doses than even the most diligent change-oriented team will have anticipated. Generally, younger members of the team will thrive on change, while some (but not all) older ones might experience some fatigue. I remember a particularly frenzied week at PricewaterhouseCoopers during which one of the senior partners lamented, "There's just too much change going on," and then a few days later, one of the participants at our Genesis Park leadership training program piped up with, "The thing we love about this firm is that it's always changing." And then her fellow participants agreed, saying, "It's never boring," and, "We're always learning something." As a leader, you need to be sensitive to how all members of the team are processing change and follow the tips above to keep the team on track.

INNOVATION

There's no formula for innovation; leaders just know they need to encourage it. Since my arrival at INSEAD, I've been impressed with how innovation is woven into the culture; it was the first MBA program to introduce a one-year model and it's the only major business school with campuses on two different continents, Europe and Asia (as well as a presence in the Middle East and an alliance with the Wharton School of the University of Pennsylvania in the United States). One thing I've learned over the years is that there's always a better way to do *anything*. Whatever your field, you should always be looking for that better way. What will come after oil? (When I was in Abu Dhabi recently, I was amazed that this oil-producing nation – one with decent reserves – is already investing in renewable energy!) What will come after space? What will follow the Internet? What will be the next development that will change the way we work and live? Every organization should focus on the next generation of their product or service, whether it's the delivery method, the sales method, or the product or service itself.

Ideally, your organization will take the lead in innovation, and the competition will try to catch up, but this won't always be the case. That's why it's critical to track what your competition is doing at all times. But I don't advise simply following them; instead, look at the market to see why they launched their innovation and then take it to the next level. The up side in playing catch-up is that when there's a competitive threat, your team's buy-in will always come more easily. It's also critical to study the market independent of your competition. Go out and talk to customers – conduct focus groups and surveys – and ask them what products and services they really need. These conversations can provide the ideas that will underlie your next innovations.

The most critical time for innovation is when the market no longer values what you are offering; then, you innovate or die. At this point, though, there's much less chance of success because the pressure will be so intense and you won't have the time to weather a few failures before you hit on an idea that works. So it's important for the organization to keep churning out new ideas and to encourage the whole team to bring their ideas forward – and it's the leader who will create the organizational culture that will make this happen.

Just be smart about it. I recall a case at Pricewaterhouse-Coopers in the 1990s, during the early days of the Internet. Someone proposed a new product: security systems to ensure the identities of the parties to online transactions. It was a great idea, but ultimately not for us. Technology was not our core competency and not something we could invest in to the extent that the project required. As a result, we didn't have the staying power or the deep technical expertise and we wound up selling at a loss. We had identified an unmet need correctly, however, and it was eventually satisfied by others.

A few more rules for innovation:

■ **Stick to your competency.** An auto maker shouldn't be producing movies any more than an accounting firm should design Internet security systems. It's true that many of the mergers and acquisitions of the past had companies moving far outside their competencies but, in most cases, the results were poor. It rarely happens anymore, and with good reason.

■ **Focus on goods and services that you can bring to market or that you can sell to someone else** to bring to market. If you don't have access to capital, don't try to innovate in a capital-intensive area.

■ **Understand the regulatory and competitive issues surrounding your idea** before spending money on it, especially if you plan to sell it internationally. Here, I'm not talking about environmental, consumer or other regulations that would restrict your product (although it's important to have a handle on those), but on regulatory situations that can protect your idea – or not. China has become rather notorious for its lack of laws to protect intellectual property, so if your product could be copied there, it's important to make other protective measures part of your marketing plan (antipiracy encryption features, for example). These will likely only buy you a few months before the intellectual property thieves figure out how to get around them, but a few months can give you the head-start you need to get established in the marketplace.

- **Don't hesitate to undertake a joint venture**. The pharmaceutical companies have done this extremely well, and it has allowed them to diversify their research and increase their hit rate dramatically. (Of course, do your due diligence to make sure you partner with the right people.)

- **Take time to evaluate each project on a regular basis** and reconsider whether to stay the course, make changes or get out altogether. This will help to ensure that you are not throwing good money on a failing proposition. You often hear the phrase "grow or die". But you can't define growth as "top line growth" only. It's possible – and often it's necessary – to shrink an organization to make it more profitable and poised for greater growth in the future.

Innovation can be a threatening proposition. As a leader, you must be aware that if you're really innovating, chances are you are throwing out a lot of established practice and wisdom. This can be a scary thing, particularly in a multicultural environment where the fear of being wrong is matched only by the fear of being right. If the competitive situation allows, the transcultural leader can manage the situation so that everything doesn't happen at once – so that it's a case of evolution rather than revolution. You don't have to overhaul everything at the same time, only the things that will differentiate your product or service.

Whatever the pace of your innovation program, the best way I know of to deal with the fears of team members is through regular and open communication. Ask people how they're doing. What are they worried about? What feels good? How can the leader help? You'll communicate a sense of empathy for the team and get early warning of problems and opportunities, so you can address them on a timely basis.

A final thought about change and innovation: The most difficult change for a leader to implement has nothing to do with products, delivery systems, customer service or back office practices. The most difficult thing to change is culture. What if you are recruited or promoted to lead a change in culture? This is one of those times when you might want to recall my warning about not being too idealistic. A board, or the CEO, or the top partners might know their organization needs to change, but when it comes down to it, they might lack the will or the heart to do so. So I would never take on an assignment for an organization in need of major culture change without doing lots of due diligence. You have to look people in the eye and say, "Here is what is needed. Are you up for it? Will you support it with resources, time, training and whatever else is required?"

Likewise, if you are an aspiring leader, you need to assess your surroundings carefully. If you are in an environment that doesn't accept change and doesn't embrace people who try to make things better, then perhaps you should look for another job. Before you do, however, share your concerns with a mentor outside the company, and see what he or she thinks. Assess yourself: If you find yourself feeling like you have all the answers, all the good ideas, if only somebody would listen, you have, my friend, succumbed to ego and need to work on your attitude. Be honest. Are you in a place where change happens, where people listen to you and ask for your ideas and respect your opinions? If so, even if you don't "sell" all your ideas, you're in an environment that values change. If not, you need to work on your long-range plan.

The millennial generation – those who graduated in 2000 or later – will be much more professionally mobile than their parents, and more willing to seek out their own opportunities. If they find themselves in organizations that are unwilling to change and innovate, they will move on, and those organizations will die because they will lose their young talent. It's as simple as that.

11

LEADERSHIP IN TIMES OF CRISIS

The Chinese word for crisis has two characters: crisis and opportunity. That's something for the transcultural leader to keep in mind. In times of crisis, the leader's actions (or lack thereof) can cause things to deteriorate further, or they can make a bad situation better. Consider the response of the US federal government to the devastation caused by Hurricane Katrina in the Mississippi River basin. The so-called emergency systems failed horribly, and despite the outpouring of support from the world, those in charge seemed confused, ineffectual, distant, operating in self-preservation mode or all of the above. Contrast that with the behavior of Rudolph Giuliani, then mayor of New York City, when the World Trade Center was destroyed by terrorists in 2001. On the face of it, there wasn't much that could be done, again despite the outpouring of support from a shocked world. The towers were down and the race was on to dig out the few survivors. But Giuliani was on the scene, tireless, compassionate, consistent and available. A leader can only hope never to have to deal with a crisis of the magnitude of 9/11, but Giuliani can provide a model for how to conduct oneself should the worst happen in whatever venue you are operating in.

To be sure, "grace under pressure" is not the only component of leadership in crisis. I could say it's just the beginning, but actually it's the end, the final step. I divide crisis leadership into two distinct parts: planning and reaction. The former begins long before a crisis ever happens. The latter goes into play when a crisis takes place.

As always, both become complicated when you are dealing in a multicultural environment. Take planning: you can't plan for crisis unless you acknowledge that your organization is fallible and, yes, that a crisis might happen. That might sound obvious, but I once had a discussion with a group from around the world about crisis management in business, and what emerged was that all the non-Americans in the group were convinced that a crisis was something that only happened in America! This was shortly after the revelations of fraud and mismanagement at Enron and Worldcom. When I mentioned that a similar debacle had taken place at Ahold, a Dutch company, they replied that Ahold's American subsidiary was responsible for the problem, which only proved their point. Two or three weeks later, the Parmalat fraud hit the headlines – a purely European scandal. I sent off a few articles about it to my colleagues with a note that said, "I rest my case."

Reaction to crisis likewise means different things in different cultures. In some Asian countries, the proper thing to do is to take responsibility for what has transpired and resign. By contrast, in the United States, some CEOs might acknowledge the situation but deny any personal wrongdoing, and try to hang on by their fingernails until they are forced out. Political conditions also have a huge impact on how a culture responds to a crisis. Where the free flow of information is not a cultural value, those in power might try to deny that a crisis exists. (Witness the initial attempts of the Chinese government to deny that many citizens were infected with the AIDS virus several years ago, due to lack of sanitary procedures employed in blood drives.)

My point is that you can't assume everyone will naturally recognize and respond to a crisis in the same way. It's important for the transcultural leader to have this in mind when planning for crisis, sounding the alarm and managing the response.

PLANNING FOR CRISIS

Whether you call it crisis planning or less dramatically, scenario planning, as it's known in some quarters, it's vital for a leader to spend some time thinking about the various negative possibilities and plan how the organization will deal with them. I always ask executives whether they've done their scenario planning, and I'm amazed at how often the answer is no or, if yes, how superficial the plan is. A good leader will take crisis planning seriously.

- **Assemble a team:** Scenario planning is best done by a diverse team drawn from all segments and functions of the organization, maybe a dozen people or so, depending on the size of the organization. Like any other team the leader assembles, this one should be diverse in age, gender, business area, culture and other characteristics. At the start, they should meet regularly for a few months.

- **Evaluate the risks:** The team should analyze the kinds of risks that the organization faces, both internal and external: natural disasters or terrorist acts that can bring operations to a standstill; managerial fraud or error that can make the numbers look good when they're not; or product failure, equipment error, consumer tampering or employee sabotage, all of which can cause customers to stop buying and hurt the organization's reputation and its standing in the marketplace. The team should also consider the competition, the regulatory environment, the economic conditions and political situations in the countries where the organization has an interest, and whatever other areas might pose a risk. These will be different in every organization. The point is to walk through as many as possible and challenge the easy assumptions.

- **Draft an emergency plan and eliminate obvious risks:** You can't plan for every contingency, but you can try to come close. Walk through various scenarios, formulate an overall emergency plan, set up chains of command and communication and make back-up plans should your "Plan A" prove to be unworkable. Draft general emergency plans for various kinds of crises (one for natural disasters, another for product tampering, for example). You should also eliminate obvious risks. Example: One company that was particularly hard hit on 9/11 had its main computer system and its back-up system located within three blocks of one another in lower Manhattan, and both were destroyed. Other companies had their back-up facilities outside New York, and they were able to resume operations more quickly.

- **Communicate with the rest of the organization:** The scenario-planning team should be known and accessible to everyone in the organization, so that anyone at any level can contribute ideas, information and observations. Once the plan is drafted, everyone in the organization should be familiar with the crisis plan – alternative work locations, back-up computer systems, who is authorized to talk to the press and so on – so that if the worst happens, they know what to do.

- **Reassess the risks and update the plans on a regular basis:** Once the initial scenario planning is done, the team should continue to meet, quarterly or as necessary, to reassess the plan, identify new risks and analyze new information. Too often, an emergency plan is written and filed away, untouched for years, until a crisis hits. By then the plan is out of date.

While it's important to establish a formal scenario-planning team and keep it focused, I also believe that the leader has a special role to play in crisis prevention. Call it early intervention, if you like. As I've said, the true transcultural leader is in touch with what's going on in the organization globally on a day-to-day basis, not micromanaging, but getting the big picture. This view is ideal for spotting trends – and that's just what some crises are. We're accustomed to thinking of crises as single events – tsunamis, power grid failures, whatever – but many are domino-like trends that begin small and, if unchecked, grow to threaten the entire organization. What I mean is that most of the time, the leader won't be faced with a burning building, but instead will have to deal with lots of "burning platforms". If you can pick up on a dangerous trend or burning platform early, you can take steps to prevent disaster.

In my experience, the signals are often subtle, but they frequently involve loss of some kind. Leaders should be sensitive to:

- Loss of talent (top people)
- Loss of market share and/or key customers; loss of credibility in the marketplace

- Loss of energy, enthusiasm by the team

- Loss of pride by the team – "organizational malaise" if you will

- Loss of money

It might work this way: You notice that your top competitor has hired away two of your best performers. You immediately try to find out why they left. Perhaps the competitor has a new product that your team and the market think is better and more exciting than what your organization is offering. Perhaps the competitor is trying to lure away your best clients by poaching your talent. When you figure out what's going on, you can work with the team to head off the crisis.

One other thing about a leader's approach to crisis planning: It's always wise to listen to the whistleblowers – the people within the organization who try to alert the higher-ups to potential problems. This can be difficult. Psychologists who have studied the whistleblower phenomenon tell us that these individuals can be loners, ornery types who have a streak of self-righteousness and a single-minded approach to life. But LINOs who ignore whistleblowers imperil themselves and their organizations. In too many cases, when whistleblowers have been silenced, penalized or fired, the consequences have been costly, tragic or both. Remember, listening is the most important trait of a leader. It doesn't matter who the speaker is or what the issue is; if you dismiss it without investigating, you play with fire. (On the other hand, if it turns out that the whistleblower is not a whistleblower at all, but a disgruntled individual who wants to harm the organization, you must deal with the person forcefully and decisively – both as discipline for the individual and as an example to others.)

REACTING TO CRISIS

If you've done your scenario planning, you will have a road map to guide your reaction to a crisis. While you might have to revise it as you go, at least you'll have the framework. But reacting to a crisis is much more complex than following a plan, however well made.

You could say that a crisis is the test of the leader. It will call upon every skill and technique you've worked so hard to acquire. Besides relying on the team you've put together, you'll be communicating – listening and speaking both; using your network; setting goals and making decisions in real time; and relying on your executive presence to project accountability, confidence, calm and compassion in whatever proportions are necessary. As the leader, you (and perhaps a select few others) will personify the organization and its reaction to the crisis; depending on the nature of the crisis, it will fall to you to reassure the stakeholders: clients and customers, your team and their families, the financial markets, the media and the public. There are a few things to remember:

- **Transparent communications:** In times of crisis, people are fearful and angry. The leader must communicate honestly and often with the appropriate stakeholders to explain what is known about the problem and how the organization will solve it. If not, the fearful and angry will manufacture explanations for what has happened, point fingers, construct conspiracy theories and gossip wildly, all of which will only make the problem worse.

  One other thought on the subject of communications, and this is something the leader should keep in mind at all times, but particularly in times of crisis: the media. It's vital for a leader to understand how to deal with media professionals, who in today's world can range from newspaper, radio and TV reporters to bloggers to private citizens with cell-phone cameras. It's commonplace to criticize the media for going after sensational news, but the truth is that they (a) have a job to do and (b) vary as widely in their motivation and approach as used-car salespeople, lawyers and even leaders/LINOs. Some are professional and honorable and the others... are the others. In a crisis, you can't control whom you'll talk to. It's easy to get into a conversation, get boxed into a corner – and then it's too late. So you need to prepare for media encounters in a crisis. In your scenario planning, designate who, besides yourself, is authorized to speak for the organization, and make sure everybody else knows how to gracefully refer all inquiries to those spokespeople. For the spokespeople, including yourself, media training is very useful, and there are lots of consultants out there, many veteran media people, who can teach you how the media works and help you practice your skills and use the media to get your message out. (The Internet is ideal in a crisis, because you can communicate your message with immediacy and know it will reach a worldwide audience.) The bottom line is this: You can never assume you're "off the record". If you do, someone will take advantage of you.

- **Decisive direction and action:** A crisis is a time for action, not introspection. This is not to say that planning and thought are unnecessary; of course they are. But time is of the essence. In the course of business, a true leader has mastered the art of convening the team to gather information, weigh the options, make decisions, craft a plan of action and implement it; now is the time to put all those functions into overdrive.

- **Involvement and presence:** A time of crisis is one time that delegation is a bad idea. The leader must be front and center, communicating the organization's message, meeting with stakeholders and constituents. At such times, the leader is the voice and face of the organization. He or she is also the motivator of the team. Yes, they'll derive their energy and sense of mission from the crisis itself and from the sense of "all being in this together". But you will bolster that energy and drive if can you show them that their leader is "in it" with them, that you are prepared to get your hands dirty and that you have confidence in their ability to solve the problem.

- **Accountability:** I like to put it this way: Share the glory but take the blame. When the organization performs heroically to solve or mitigate a crisis, the leader must credit the team. But if the organization is at fault, the responsibility for what happened and how to fix it ultimately belongs to the leader. Any attempt to shift the blame is a bad idea and will undermine the leader's credibility and effectiveness – and it will also demoralize the team and interfere with their attempts to execute the action plan. Sadly, we see this kind of finger-pointing all the time in politics.

When I think of leadership in a time of crisis, I come back to two words: confidence and compassion. Compassion comes into play when there is loss of life, physical injury or devastating loss of property (by this I mean anything from the obliteration of people's homes by Hurricane Katrina to the disappearance of their retirement funds in the Enron

105

debacle). At such times, the leader must – as good leaders and good people naturally will – show sensitivity. He or she must not seem aloof or unmoved by the losses taking place. But at the same time, a leader in despair, who lacks confidence, will only make a bad situation worse. The leader must be able to "rally the troops" and to give hope. I have to return to the example of Mayor Giuliani here. Each time he appeared on camera in those terrible hours and days after 9/11, he projected a near-perfect balance of compassion for the losses suffered by so many and confidence that New York would ultimately prevail. I think the city's resiliency and its recovery is owing in part to his leadership. And that's what it's all about.

12

WORK-LIFE BALANCE

When I was growing up, my dad went off to work at the bank every day, and my mom was home running the household and taking care of me and my brother, Bob. Dad spent most of his days at the bank, but his hours were pretty regular, and on his days off he taught me how to fish and play golf and took me to hockey games – we were big hockey fans! Mom saw us off to school every morning and was there with a smile and a hug every afternoon; in between, she saw to all the little details that make a household run smoothly. That was how things went in the 1960s and early 1970s in suburban America. Of course, there were some kids who didn't get to spend as much time with their dads because those dads put in extra hours at the office, and there were other kids whose moms worked outside the home. But it seems to me that because gender roles were more rigidly defined then, achieving a balance between work and the rest of life was easier.

Looking back, it's hard to believe what a profound change took place in the course of just a few years. When middle-class women began to enter the workforce in large numbers, the traditional arrangement that had worked so well for legions of Joe and Elizabeth Browns gave way to a world of new and different ones. It happened in my own life, when my wife, Susan, decided to go back to school and get her law degree. She had worked for two years as a paralegal, but

107

since we both came from traditional families, she had quit her job to stay at home when our first child, Chris, was born. When our second child, Sarah, was still quite young, Susan decided that she wanted to apply to law school. She had always believed in me and encouraged me – she pushed me to take my CPA exam and pass it, and she supported me in all my subsequent professional efforts – so I felt happy and privileged to help her pursue her dream. We were still in our twenties and we didn't have a lot of money, but we looked into the loan programs and made it work. For three years, Susan went to law school full time. We had babysitters for the kids on weekdays and we had me (when I wasn't traveling) at night and on weekends. And we continued juggling back and forth once she started to practice law. Like countless other families then and to this day, we figured out how to balance work and the rest of life.

And because it wasn't a given, because we had to make it up as we went along, I became very aware of how much "the rest of life" meant to me. In those early years, our babysitter budget was limited and if I had a deadline that obliged me to work over the weekend, instead of getting a sitter, I brought the kids to the office with me. (Sweet memories: When my son was five or six years old, he told his teacher his father's job consisted of "numbers and pictures". That's because when he came to the office, I gave him colored pens to draw with and a ten-key calculator to play with! Another time, I brought Sarah to visit a client who made bubble gum. She loved it – what kid wouldn't? – and I was a hero for the day.) Looking back, I'm so glad I made the effort – and had the support of my superiors – to bring the kids along when I had to, to attend the school concerts, the sporting events, the parent-teacher conferences, the birthday parties and all the rest. How precious it was – and still is.

Over the years, society developed a name for this kind of juggling act: work-life balance. And it shocks me that so many people are still struggling with it – and that includes singles and couples, people with kids and without. It's a challenge for everyone. Indeed, with periodic staff down-sizings that make workloads grow proportionately, and round-the-clock electronic access that can interrupt just about anything at any time, work-life balance is harder than ever to achieve. Not that you can punch in at 9 a.m. and out at 5 p.m. and become a CEO (or even close); in our competitive world, a leader or aspiring leader can expect to put in 50 to 60 hours a week. But I believe that making time for a life outside work is critical for everyone, from the leader down to the most junior member of the staff. The alternative – a job that takes up 100 per cent of your time, that *becomes* your life – results in burn-out, exhaustion and dissatisfaction, not to mention the loss of all those wonderful minutes and hours spent with loved ones, or growing your garden, or listening to opera, or watching a football game or whatever it is that nourishes your soul. From a business perspective, having led many teams over the years, I can report that the person who has a fulfilling life outside of work is the person who also shines at work. These days, when many organizations are under pressure to "do more with less", it can be easy to get sucked into the habit of working too much, staying too long at the office, bringing work home – and not just on a short-term basis, but on every project, every time. And it can be easy for the LINO to look the other way and let it happen. This is a mistake. It might result in greater productivity in the short term, but leaders, as we've said, must consider the long term. The true leader will take pains to make work-life balance a reality for every member of the team, including himself or herself.

Of course, work-life balance means different things in different cultures. In the US, too often, vacation is what you fit in when there's nothing major going on at the office. And it's likely that you check e-mails and voice mails while you're away. Some people are almost ashamed to take their vacation time, as though it's a sign of weakness. In Europe, vacations, or holidays, as they're called, are sacred. Nobody deviates from a planned holiday unless there's a crisis taking place. I heartily endorse the European model! Take the vacation you are due when it is due, and don't apologize. Don't be shy, either. Schedule it in advance, tell the boss and/or the team about it and when you get back, show your pictures and tell your stories. It's part of life and it's part of work. It's especially important for the leader to take a vacation, as it sets a good example for the rest of the team.

The transcultural leader should also be aware of other work-life differences among cultures. The early-to-bed-and-early-to-rise ethic of the US business scene couldn't be further from that of some Latin cultures, where dinner doesn't get under way until at least 10 p.m. and continues for hours, sometimes into the morning. Late-night partying after dinner is obligatory in some Asian countries as well. I remember a transaction we worked on between a Korean company and an American one. We were working at a hotel near the American company's headquarters in a small town in the Midwestern United States. The due diligence team from the Korean company consisted of just five people and I was their advisor. They had asked for an 8 a.m. meeting every morning to check in and get a briefing on the progress of the deal. One day, they didn't show up at 8 o'clock. Or 8:15. Or 8:30. We finally called up to one of their rooms and it was obvious that we woke the fellow up. He must have awakened the rest of the team, and soon they came down, one by one, all looking a bit ashen, and we commenced our meeting. Afterward, I pulled the youngest one aside – he spoke the best English – and asked what had happened. He apologized profusely and said they had driven to Chicago (an hour away) and had sampled the city's nightlife. The poor guy had been the designated driver. Their night out was clearly an important part of their stay in the United States, and if I had known they wanted to do it, I'd have set up a car service and rescheduled the day's work for a slightly later hour, so that we could have our morning briefing before getting back to the negotiating table.

There are other work-life issues to be aware of when doing business in a multicultural setting. In the United States, a working lunch might easily be sandwiches delivered to the conference table, the better to keep working. This would be unthinkably uncivilized in some European countries, where lunch is a true break from work, and anything less is insulting. Likewise, the length of the business day and the length of the workweek will vary from place to place. When conducting business away from home or dealing with people from another culture, the transcultural leader would do well to find out what the work-life expectations are before setting any schedules.

But those are the easy things. The real challenge for the leader comes in looking out for your own and your team's work-life balance while making sure that the work of the organization gets done. This can mean making allowances for the young family in which both parents (or the single parent) work outside the home. It can also mean giving some leeway to the woman whose elderly mother is seriously ill. Or the man who periodically comes in late because he is getting chemotherapy. In some cases, these situations will be governed by law or by company policy. In others, it will be up to you, the leader. My view is that families come first, and sickness will happen. Most of the time you can work around it; if you show concern for the team member's challenges and troubles, he or she will likely work even harder when things return to normal. If the team member is chronically absent and unable to do the job, then it's time for a serious discussion. Once again, the key here is open communication.

As a leader, you can make it clear that on your watch, there will be no such thing as "face time". That is, you won't have the team putting in long hours just to show their faces. I've seen situations in which the team members don't leave as long as the boss is in the office because they're fearful of being seen going out the door before he does. That's ridiculous. I've always subscribed to the theory that professionals know their jobs and know what they need to do to get them done. Normal business hours usually suffice, and in situations when a tough deadline demands that they put in extra hours, they'll know it and behave accordingly. But I never want people to hang around just because I'm in the building.

The flip side of face time is the too-heavy workload. Especially when companies downsize staff, workloads can become demanding. Too often, those who have engineered the downsizing stop there, without regard to the effect on the people who remain. From what I have seen, most organizations do not take the time to reengineer jobs. It's incumbent on the leader to help the team prioritize the work at hand, to look periodically at what's being done versus what is really needed. And leaders must look at the work with an open mind, to identify what is critical to the organization's current strategic plan and what can be left undone until time allows.

It's also incumbent on the team members, the aspiring leaders, to communicate with the leader when the workload becomes too intense, but this can only happen when the leader has cultivated an atmosphere in which communication is free, open and continual. If team members fear recriminations because an e-mail sent at 9 p.m. isn't answered the same night, chances are they don't have confidence that their workplace will respect work-life balance or work-life boundaries. (Of course, if there's an emergency at 9 p.m., a leader will have crafted a system for letting the team know and getting the necessary response.) Under normal circumstances, I don't want people taking work home and working all night. I want every member of my team to have a life. I want them to feel confident in saying, "I've had enough for the day; I'm going home." I want them to know how to prioritize, to identify what's critical and what can wait and, above all, to communicate those things to others on the team and to me.

I want to stress that if the leader honestly opens the lines of communication, then the members of the team must take responsibility and speak up. I've seen many a talented individual become frustrated and resentful over a situation he or she could easily have controlled if only he or she had spoken up. Learning to say no is one of the most important milestones in your professional development. If you have a full plate, say so. If he or she's smart, the boss won't want you to commit to something you can't handle. Finesse the situation by saying something like this: "I'd love to help, but I have already committed to these three tasks. Is there one that is less pressing so I can free up some time to do what you are asking?" If you have an outside commitment and your boss asks you to do something extra that will require you to work, be honest and say, "I have plans for that weekend that I would really like to keep." Most bosses will respect this and will only push back when the need is really critical.

I also want to stress that, as in so many other areas, the leader can't wait for the team members to speak up about work-life balance. Even when the leader has nurtured an environment of terrific give-and-take about work-life issues, some people will always be reticent about saying anything negative about work-life demands – especially if the team is a multicultural one. This is discouraging if you take it personally, because it implies that the leader doesn't care and that the situation is so far gone it's not worth talking about. So don't take it personally and, more important, don't wait for the team to come to you; you have to be connected and you have to keep asking people how they're doing, what's good and what's bad. If you can be open and willing to solve the situation together, the team will be comfortable coming to you, not just with job-related problems, but with work-life balance issues, too.

Whether you are a leader or a junior team member, remember this: You are empowered to speak up for what you need in order to attain a reasonable and happy work-life balance. If you don't at least try, you have only yourself to blame. If you do speak up, and the organization doesn't support you, either you've asked for too much, or you're not in a place that respects the individual's need to have time for "the rest of life" and you need to think again about your long-range plan. Your mentor will help you figure out which is which. But do speak up; life's too short to wait.

13

LEADING INTO THE FUTURE

If you take leadership seriously, you've probably put so much effort into achieving your position and then doing the job as well as you possibly can that stepping out of it can seem as remote as taking a stroll on Jupiter. But I believe that every leader has a responsibility to help others to succeed – even if that means "to succeed" the leader himself or herself. Indeed, a true leader is honor-bound to do some serious succession planning to ensure the health and future of the team and the organization.

As I've noted earlier, if you want to be a successful leader, protecting your own position can't be your first priority. This is just as true when you are preparing for the future as it is in your day-to-day operations. For the good of the organization, you have to prepare to let go. This can be uncomfortable for those who lack confidence or are afflicted with political paranoia. And it's not only the LINOs who fail to plan for the next generation. Even the most passionate and visionary leaders can get so caught up in leading that they never quite get around to grooming a successor. Witness the arts organizations that have withered away when the founding artist has died or become too old to carry on.

Because I've held a number of leadership positions in my career, I've done my share of succession planning. I can recall one instance when I decided to move to a new challenge after leading the globalization of the merger and acquisition business at PricewaterhouseCoopers. It had been an exciting position, but the opportunity arose to move to an equally challenging post, and I jumped at it. I narrowed the field of candidates and, as it happened, the ideal person to be my successor was my second-in-command. He was ready, willing and able. He was British – a nice counterpoint to my American roots – and we had worked together for a few years and had really built a diverse and talented team together. As a result, the handover was fairly seamless; he was very successful in the role and the team continued to thrive. The best thing about the transition was that he brought a different perspective to the business, but at the same time he was able to relate to the people who had been working with us before. He very considerately invited me to participate in meetings and events from time to time. When I saw that he was making changes, I held my tongue and, on reflection, realized that they were all for the better. I took my own advice: If you do succession right, it means letting go, and allowing someone else to "bring up your baby"!

Make no mistake: when you've built a team or an organization, it's not easy to pass the baton. But I've always believed a leader must plan for the future and I've never feared the consequences. And in every leadership post I've held, I've made a point to surround myself with good people and identify at least two successors for my job. A little secret: This has not only been good organizationally, but it's been good for me as well. It's one of those areas where my big-picture philosophy has converged nicely with my personal "likes": I like to develop other people and I like to do different things. Looking back, I'm happy to say that I've been able to do a lot more in my career because there has always been someone ready to step into my job when I've been ready to move

on to something else. And my successors have all made me
proud.

That's because my succession candidates earned their status. In my view, a transcultural leader shouldn't pick his or
her replacement based on friendship or cronyism. The good
of the organization depends on picking the best person for
the job. But that's not always the guiding philosophy of those
who must choose the leader for the next generation. In some
cultures, succession is almost a birthright, rather than a prize
to be earned through talent and hard work. This is particularly true in societies that aren't democratic and open. The
autocratic management style that characterizes such places
tends to bleed from politics into other areas, ensuring that
most successions are based on the whim or paranoia of the
departing chief executive – or the committee that has removed
him. (Succession can also be considered a birthright in organizations where the founder or founding family is active. This
can be a questionable practice, but it can succeed when the
family member is selected because he or she is the right person with the right skills. If those aren't the selection criteria,
the results can be disastrous.) When you are operating in
cultures that regard succession as a birthright, or something
to be decided in secret by a select few, crafting a succession
plan based on merit, in an atmosphere of transparency and
openness, might seem revolutionary. This is the kind of situation in which the transcultural leader should proceed
with caution and tact. In some places, age is the first deter-
minant of succession. In countries such as China, India, Japan
and parts of Europe, it can be tough for someone under 50
(or even older) to get to the top unless they are entrepre-
neurs; it just doesn't happen in established organizations.
In recent years, however, as companies in these countries join
the public markets and feel the pressure of accountability,

succession has become more merit-driven. Even so, the trans-cultural leader will tread carefully here, so as not to offend. In cultures that revere seniority, it might not be wise, for example, to tap people as candidates for succession too early in their careers. This shouldn't be a problem if your team consists of top people of all ages.

Even in cultures where public markets mandate that executives and their governing boards be accountable to shareholders, the LINOs of the world have seen to it that succession-by-cronyism has crept into the process. In recent years, a surge of shareholder movements questioning CEO performance and their compensation packages has under-scored the need for leaders to guard against any succession appointment that isn't based on merit. Each case will be different, and the global markets are changing so quickly that, in some cultures, rules that once seemed carved into the bedrock are being revised. As with any issue, the trans-cultural leader will do the due diligence and find out what's happening "on the ground" and then craft a succession plan that takes local customs into account even as it adheres to the values of transparency and meritocracy. What I have found is that you can usually win people over to your way of thinking if you engage and consult with them: Commu-nicate with them, walk them through the process, explain why it is important and hear their thoughts – and fears, if that's the case. As with so many of the other leadership issues discussed in this book, if you can make your team feel as though they are part of the process, as though your plan is their plan, they will generally buy in. When I accepted my current position at INSEAD, I told the board that one of my goals would be to build a strong team, from which possible successors would one day emerge. As of this writing, I'm still looking forward to my first anniversary in the job, but I've already concluded that there are a lot of talented people at INSEAD. That might seem early to start succession planning, but the truth is that "phase one" begins when you assemble your first team. Surround yourself with the brightest talent and the most diverse collection of cultures and backgrounds that you can, and you're on your way. Give your team members challenging assignments and let them shine, and you've taken another step. LINOs tend to let talented people labor in the background so they don't emerge as potential successors, but true leaders give their teams enough responsibility to show all that they can do. This is true when you begin the job, and each time you put together a team thereafter.

Besides building strong teams, the transcultural leader should encourage team members to learn and internalize all the principles we've covered thus far – respect for openness, transparency and diversity; reliance on talented teams and thorough due diligence to set and achieve high goals and make decisions; regard for the importance of change, innovation and preparedness for crisis; and admiration of merit and achievement. The leader should also push the transcultural "ethic" and encourage aspiring leaders, as well as all team members, to get as much international experience as they can and learn at least one language beyond their mother tongue.

If you have done your work as a leader, by the time you are ready to think seriously about succession, you will know who the candidates are. Chances are, because your team is already multicultural, the short list of candidates will be, too – and you won't feel the pressure to be politically correct when you create your candidate list. Your best and brightest will be culturally diverse because you've designed your team that way from the outset.

Once you've got your short list, I'd break the process into a series of steps:

- Place each candidate in a responsible and visible position.
- Give all of them the opportunity to succeed (or fail).
- Be honest and open with them and others about the process.
- Make your decision.

One of the best-known succession plans played out in 2001, when Jack Welch was retiring as CEO of GE. He had identified three very strong candidates, and he put each in a position that would demonstrate their abilities. He made sure that the process was transparent and the timing of the decision was known to all, well in advance. These measures probably alleviated some of the politics surrounding what must have been an incredibly charged situation (although the three probably still felt the politics of the thing). In the end, only one of the three – Jeffrey Immelt – got the job. The other two went on to executive positions at different companies and their professional stars have risen and fallen over time. In my view, his plan was somewhat flawed because his short list was not diverse. But he has been widely, and rightfully, lauded as a high-profile leader who planned carefully for his succession, conducted the transition transparently and started well in advance. In fact, his plan and his execution of it have become the stuff of legend in the business world.

One of the things that Welch did, and that I would always recommend, is to have more than one candidate in a succession plan. Why? To be blunt, you need multiple candidates in case one falls ill or dies – or makes a bad judgment or steps out of the running for any reason. And, too, having more than one candidate during the period before you make your final decision gives you an opportunity to compare their performance, to see how they react in different situations. Three is the optimum number, in my view, because that way there isn't just one winner and one loser.

Developing leaders is good for the organization. When you build a team in which everyone starts out as a potential leader and everyone is encouraged to "live" the culture of transcultural leadership, the organization can only be better for it, no matter who is ultimately chosen as your successor.

A final thought: LINOs worry about their legacies. How will they be remembered? What will people say about them? To be honest, leaders worry about their legacies, too – they're human, after all. Who doesn't want to be remembered as having done a good job? But I contend that if you concentrate on applying the principles of transcultural leadership – including succession – every day, day in and day out, you won't have to worry about your legacy. It will take care of itself.

INDEX